Reinventing Cities for People and the Planet

MOLLY O'MEARA

Jane A. Peterson, *Editor*

WORLDWATCH PAPER 147

June 1999

THE WORLDWATCH INSTITUTE is an independent, nonprofit environmental research organization in Washington, DC. Its mission is to foster a sustainable society in which human needs are met in ways that do not threaten the health of the natural environment or future generations. To this end, the Institute conducts interdisciplinary research on emerging global issues, the results of which are published and disseminated to decision-makers and the media.

FINANCIAL SUPPORT for the Institute is provided by the Geraldine R. Dodge Foundation, the Ford Foundation, the William and Flora Hewlett Foundation, W. Alton Jones Foundation, Charles Stewart Mott Foundation, the Curtis and Edith Munson Foundation, David and Lucile Packard Foundation, V. Kann Rasmussen Foundation, Rockefeller Financial Services, Summit Foundation, Turner Foundation, U.N. Population Fund, Wallace Genetic Foundation, Wallace Global Fund, Weeden Foundation, and the Winslow Foundation. The Institute also receives financial support from its Council of Sponsors members—Tom and Cathy Crain, Toshishige Kurosawa, Kazuhiko Nishi, Roger and Vicki Sant, Robert Wallace, and Eckart Wintzen—and from the Friends of Worldwatch.

THE WORLDWATCH PAPERS provide in-depth, quantitative and qualitative analysis of the major issues affecting prospects for a sustainable society. The Papers are written by members of the Worldwatch Institute research staff and reviewed by experts in the field. Published in five languages, they have been used as concise and authoritative references by governments, nongovernmental organizations, and educational institutions worldwide. For a partial list of available Papers, see back pages.

REPRINT AND COPYRIGHT INFORMATION for one-time academic use of this material is available by contacting Customer Service, Copyright Clearance Center, at (978) 750-8400 (phone), or (978) 750-4744 (fax), or writing to CCC, 222 Rosewood Drive, Danvers, MA 01923. Nonacademic users should call the Worldwatch Institute's Communication Department at (202) 452-1992, x517, or fax a request to (202) 296-7365.

Table of Contents

Introduction 5

An Urbanizing World 12

Closing the Water and Waste Circuits 17

Toward Greater Self-Reliance in Food and Energy 31

Linking Transportation and Land Use 40

Financing the Sustainable City 53

Building Political Strength 60

Appendix 69

Notes 77

Tables and Figures

Table 1: *Population of World's 10 Largest Metropolitan Areas
in 1000, 1800, and 1900, with Projections for 2000* 14

Table 2: *Rate and Scale of Population Growth in Selected Industrial
Cities, 1875–1900, and Developing Cities, 1975–2000* 16

Table 3: *Transportation Indicators in Selected Cities,
Regional Average, 1990* 45

Figure 1: *Urban Population in Industrial and Developing Regions,
Selected Years* 17

Figure 2: *Annual Per Capita Car Use in Selected Cities,
by Regional Average, 1970–90* 42

Figure 3: *Sources of Local Revenue, Average of Selected Cities
Worldwide, 1993* 55

Map: *The World at Night, 1994–95* 10

Map: *World's Largest Cities and Most Rapidly Urbanizing
Countries, 1995* 18

ACKNOWLEDGMENTS: Thanks to Peter Newman, Haynes Goddard, Rutherford Platt, and Charlotte Allen for their helpful reviews of an earlier incarnation of this paper. I am also indebted to Chris Calwell, Bob McNulty, David Painter, David Rain, and Don Chen for their invaluable comments on this version. And thanks to Chris Elvidge, Jeff Kenworthy, Mike Ratcliffe, Hiroichi Kawashima, and Christine Kessides for their kind help with data and information.

Many at Worldwatch boosted the quality of this paper. In particular, Chris Flavin helped strengthen the drafts from start to finish, Jane Peterson wielded an expert editing pen, and David Roodman dispatched advice from Vietnam. Lori Brown and Anne Smith unearthed countless books and datasets, and all of my fellow researchers offered feedback on an early draft. Sandra Postel supplied insight on water issues and Brian Halweil advised me on the food discussion. As the deadline neared, Payal Sampat, Gary Gardner, Brian Halweil, Seth Dunn, and Ashley Mattoon tracked down information for key calculations. Hilary French and Lisa Mastny took time out for a last-minute discussion of the conclusions. Liz Doherty turned manuscript into flawless page proofs at breakneck speed. Dick Bell, Mary Caron, Amy Warehime, and Alison Trice did a stellar job with communications and outreach. Suzanne Clift pitched in with welcome morale boosting. And Payal Sampat and Lisa Mastny carefully proofread the final drafts.

Finally, heartfelt thanks to Jim, Clare, and Megan O'Meara for their support, and to Joe Sheehan for his patience.

MOLLY O'MEARA is a research associate at the Worldwatch Institute, where she studies the role of cities and information technology in solving environmental problems. She is a contributing author of the Institute's annual books, *State of the World* and *Vital Signs*. And she has written for *World Watch* magazine on climate change, solar power, and Asia-Pacific trade. Before joining Worldwatch in 1996, she researched science and environment stories at *Asahi Shimbun*, one of Japan's largest daily newspapers. Molly graduated from Williams College with a degree in Biology and Asian Studies.

Introduction

Seen at night from above, cities light up the continents. A satellite image of the Earth shows bright dots, the glow cast by urban centers, illuminating much of Japan, Western Europe, and the United States. Cutting across South America, a swath of darkness separates the cluster of lights at the continent's northern edge from those below the Amazon Basin. Coastal China and India shine brightly, while much of Asia's interior is dark. Australia is lit only by a string of lights on its east coast and a few dots on the west coast. The outline of Africa is similarly faint, with concentrations of brightness at the northern and southern tips. Entire land masses—Greenland, Madagascar, and Papua New Guinea—do not show up at all.[1]

City lights cover more of the planet than ever before. In 1900, only 160 million people, one tenth of the world's population, were city dwellers. By 2006, in contrast, half the world (3.2 billion people) will be living in urban areas—a 20-fold increase—and most of the growth will occur in developing countries, much of it due to the natural increase in local populations. In addition, the desperate search for employment and higher incomes will continue to propel millions of people toward the city lights as it has for a century and a half. In China alone, some 460 million people—nearly as many as now live in the United States and Indonesia combined—are expected to join the urban population by 2030.[2]

The economic and cultural advantages of cities are impressive, but so are the environmental problems they create.

As early as the 1850s, when rapid industrialization made the United Kingdom the first nation in the world to house more than half of its population in cities, Charles Dickens chronicled the ills of the industrial city. "It was a town of unnatural red and black like the painted face of a savage," he wrote in his 1854 novel *Hard Times*. "It was a town of machines and tall chimneys, out of which interminable serpents of smoke trailed themselves for ever and ever...." As the Industrial Revolution spread from the United Kingdom to continental Europe, then North America, and later Japan, these nations, too, became predominantly urban. Booming industrial cities used vast quantities of water, food, fuels, and building materials. Pollution and waste were evident everywhere.[3]

While improvements in water and sanitation have brought pollution-related illness in industrial countries down to relatively manageable levels, industrialization in the developing world in the last three decades has led to urban health problems on an unprecedented scale. Today, at least 220 million people in cities of the developing world lack clean drinking water, 420 million do not have access to the simplest latrines, 600 million do not have adequate shelter, and 1.1 billion choke on unhealthy levels of air pollution. Researchers estimate that air pollution in 36 large Indian cities killed some 52,000 people in 1995, a 28 percent increase from the early 1990s. China reported at least 3 million deaths from urban air pollution between 1994 and 1996. And a recent examination of 207 cities by the World Resources Institute ranked Mexico City, Beijing, Shanghai, Tehran, and Calcutta as the five worst in terms of exposing children to sulfur dioxide, nitrogen oxides, and particulates. Just by breathing the air in their homes and streets, these children inhale the equivalent of two packs of cigarettes each day.[4]

Today, cities affect not just the health of their inhabitants but the health of the planet. Although cities have always relied on their hinterlands for food, water, and energy, urbanites today draw more heavily on far-flung resources. London, for example, now requires roughly 58 times its land area just to supply its residents with food and timber.

Meeting the needs of everyone in the world in the same way that the needs of Londoners are met would require at least three more Earths.[5]

Cities take up just 2 percent of the world's surface but consume the bulk of key resources. Roughly 78 percent of carbon emissions from fossil fuel burning and cement manufacturing, and 76 percent of industrial wood use worldwide occur in urban areas. Some 60 percent of the planet's water that is tapped for human use goes to cities in one form or another. (About half of this water irrigates food crops for urban residents, roughly a third is used by city industry, and the remainder is for drinking and sanitation.) Carbon emissions from cities stoke the atmospheric warming that threatens to destabilize global climate, forest cutting to produce urban timber speeds the loss of biological diversity worldwide, and mounting urban thirst heightens tensions over water allocation, which threaten to spark conflicts in the next century.[6]

As these links suggest, the struggle to achieve a sustainable balance between the Earth's resource base and its human energy will be largely won or lost in the world's cities. Thus, the challenge for the next century will be to create more livable and sustainable cities by improving their environmental conditions and at the same time reducing the demands that they make on the Earth's resources.

Changes in six areas—water, waste, food, energy, transportation, and land use—are needed to meet the challenge to make cities and the vast areas they affect more viable. Some technologies and policies will be new, while others will borrow from the wealth of past urban experience. One of the guiding principles will be to reform urban systems so that they mimic the metabolism of nature. Rather than devouring water, food, energy, and processed goods without regard for the impact of its ravenous appetites, and then belching out the remains as noxious pollutants, the city could align its consumption with realistic needs, produce more of its own food and energy, and put much more of its waste to use. From Curitiba, Brazil, to Copenhagen, Denmark, citizens and local leaders are already putting these ideas into action.[7]

In many cities, water is often squandered, and waste is poorly managed. Human, agricultural, and industrial wastes are usually dumped into the same water source, making reuse of that water dangerous and cleanup costly. But forward-looking cities are now cooperating with nearby towns and villages to protect local rivers and common watersheds from pollution. By fixing leaks and otherwise promoting water efficiency, cities can make full use of a valuable resource and reduce demand on reservoirs. Recycling of water is already becoming more common, but water-short cities could make reuse of water even easier by separating household and industrial wastewater. By composting organic waste and mining trash for reusable paper, glass, and metal, cities can reduce the amount of material that enters the waste stream in the first place.

Like water, food and energy are basic urban requirements that are often brought in and distributed at great environmental and economic cost. Locally produced food and energy can make a city greener and less vulnerable to price hikes and other outside disruptions. Energy efficiency, like water conservation, is critical in designing buildings for a more sustainable city. Moreover, both food and energy can be "recycled" in various ways. When organic matter is diverted from the trash heap and composted, it can help sustain urban crops. And excess heat from electricity generation can warm buildings. Many buildings in the city of Copenhagen excel at turning waste into resource: "gray water" from kitchens and compost from household waste nourish food-producing gardens, while hot water left over from power generation heats rooms.

Buildings, however, are only part of the picture. Much wasted energy and air pollution stem from a city's failure to link transportation and land use decisions in a sensible way. Sprawling cities require not only more fuel for transportation, but also more land, building materials, water lines, roads, and other infrastructure than compact ones do. Curitiba, Brazil, has shown that even a city on a tight budget can coordinate transportation and land use to support walking, biking, and efficient public buses and to reduce the preference now given to private motorized vehicles.

Powerful economic and political forces drive environmental degradation, chaotic urbanization, and the fragmentation of cities into disparate political entities that are hard put to collaborate for the benefit of the overall urban area. And each city faces its own combination of destructive forces. For instance, national governments sometimes force local authorities to underprice services and limit their power to levy taxes. With more fiscal autonomy, cities could place higher fees on water, trash collection, and road use, and levy taxes on fossil fuels in order to bring needed funds to city bank accounts and provide incentives for green technologies and jobs.

But it is not just lack of money that constrains cities. The people and businesses committed to current wasteful patterns of development constitute a potent political constituency. With better information about the sources of local problems and greater transparency in government decisions, citizens can form a counterweight to powerful interest groups and hold their local officials accountable. New information and communication technologies are beginning to empower citizens and aid local planners. More than ever before, national and international city networks are speeding exchange of ideas on common problems between officials in different cities. When leaders discover successful solutions, they serve as inspiration to others.

The sheer size and reach of cities means that they will have a profound impact on the global environment in the 21st century—for better or worse. Cities hold the potential for much greater efficiency in water, materials, food, and energy use. Although it is not always the case today, people clustered together ought to be able to use fewer of these resources, and to recycle them with greater ease, than widely dispersed populations can. With a combination of improved planning and fiscal reform, cities can lighten their burden on the planet while at the same time improving the quality of life for their citizens.

MAP

The World at Night, 1994–95

KEY

White = radiation from human settlements

This satellite image shows lights from cities, towns, and industrial facilities. It is a
composite of 231 observations between October 1994 and March 1995.

In the late 1990s, U.S. National Geophysical Data Center scientists mapped urban areas with data from a U.S. military satellite designed in the 1970s to detect moonlit clouds. They "removed" clouds that obscured cities by picking the clearest nights over 6 months and used time-series analysis to distinguish urban lights from fires or lightening.

Source: See endnote 1.

An Urbanizing World

"The rhythm of history has been the rise, collapse, and occasional rebirth of cities," writes journalist Eugene Linden. Around 4000 B.C., farming villages in Mesopotamian river valleys grew into the world's first cities. Foremost among these settlements was the Sumerian city-state—with its elaborate temples, stratified social classes, advanced technology, extended trade, and military fortifications.[8]

Between 500 B.C. and 400 B.C., the ancient Greek "polis" emerged as a basic unit of government. A self-sufficient and self-governing city-state, the polis reached its apex in Athens. This urban society laid foundations in western philosophy, drama, and art, and introduced many modern notions of democracy. Scholar Peter Hall notes, "The Athenian state was neither 'the Republic of Athens' nor 'Attica', but 'the Athenians': the citizens were the state." Every citizen had an equal voice in local decisions.[9]

The ancient Greek city-states were "free states" open to rural dwellers; in contrast, the city-states that arose in medieval Europe had walls that formally set the town off from the countryside. Over the years, these walls were often rebuilt to accommodate larger populations, as rural dwellers sought a better life in the city and as births there began to outnumber deaths. Although cut off from country dwellers, leading merchant city-states of Europe were open to the world, emerging as the centers of the first global trading system. Historian Fernand Braudel asserts that "there was no truly *international* economy before the Hanseatic League," a network of trading cities stretching from England to the Baltic Sea.[10]

The Industrial Revolution brought the next major urban transformation, as rural inhabitants poured into cities to seek jobs in industry. In the eighteenth, nineteenth, and early twentieth centuries, industrializing cities in Europe and North America surged beyond administrative limits. In many cities, the number of people living within the political boundaries of major city centers declined, particularly after

1950, as roads and buildings continued to spread over surrounding forest and farmland.[11]

Mass-produced cars, inexpensive fuel, and government policies that promoted car travel and development outside the central cities helped create this sprawl. The most extreme examples of widely dispersed suburban "edge cities" are found in the United States, where a complex of government incentives included greater tax benefits for new construction than for improving existing buildings. By steering transportation policy toward favoring the road and the private car, the 1956 Interstate Highway Act had a powerful impact on where people lived and worked. Perhaps most important, notes Kenneth Jackson in his book *The Crabgrass Frontier*, was institutionalized racial prejudice in federal assessments on which home financing is based. This bias steered investment away from existing urban neighborhoods with one or more minority residents and toward brand new communities in the suburbs, where density was considerably lower. Between 1950 and 1990, greater Chicago's population grew by 38 percent but spread over 124 percent more land; metropolitan Cleveland's population increased by 21 percent, but the city ate up 112 percent more land.[12]

As the shape of cities has changed, so have notions about what constitutes an urban area. Today, cities swell not only from births and an influx of newcomers, but also from reclassification of rural areas. Depending on the country, urban population statistics may correspond to the political boundaries of an old city center or extend to some part of the greater metropolitan region, which may have numerous centers of employment. This paper uses the United Nations (U.N.) numbers for "urban agglomerations," which generally include the population in a city or town as well as that of the adjacent suburban fringe.[13]

Economic forces underlie the ongoing changes in the role of cities. Industrialization, whether in nineteenth-century London or twentieth-century Manila, has brought both the prospect of urban jobs and the degradation of rural areas. Whereas most of the world's jobs were in agriculture in the 1950s, by 1990, most were in services—an outgrowth of industrialization. Cities still provide a marketplace for food and other items produced in the surrounding region, but a growing number also serve as global bazaars. Telephones, satellites, and computer links are among the technologies that allow today's network of "global" cities to reach beyond their immediate hinterlands. As a result, elites in Seoul and Stockholm may have more in common with each other than with their rural compatriots. Writers such as the *Atlantic Monthly's* Robert Kaplan have suggested that the economic and political importance of city regions heralds a new era of city-states. For instance, in North America, Kaplan sees the nation-states—the United States, Canada, and Mexico— overshadowed by a loose confederation of extended metropolitan areas that happen to share the same continent. These centers lack the physical grandeur of Athens or Sparta but, like them, serve as hubs of economic activity with trade links to many parts of the globe.[14]

Much modern urban infrastructure was built in response to nineteenth-century problems in the West, which hosted the world's biggest urban areas for a brief moment in

TABLE 1

Population of World's 10 Largest Metropolitan Areas in 1000, 1800, and 1900, with Projections for 2000

1000		1800	
	(million)		
Cordova	0.45	Peking	1.10
Kaifeng	0.40	London	0.86
Constantinople	0.30	Canton	0.80
Angkor	0.20	Edo (Tokyo)	0.69
Kyoto	0.18	Constantinople	0.57
Cairo	0.14	Paris	0.55
Bagdad	0.13	Naples	0.43
Nishapur	0.13	Hangchow	0.39
Hasa	0.11	Osaka	0.38
Anhilvada	0.10	Kyoto	0.38

history. In 1800, just three of the 10 largest cities were in Europe (see Table 1); by 1900, a total of nine were in Europe and the United States; but by 2000, there will only be two in "the North." Asia, which led world urbanization between 800 and 1800, again today has half of the 10 largest cities. India is a predominantly rural country, but its urban population alone—256 million—would constitute the world's fourth most populous nation.[15]

With North America, Europe, and Japan already highly urbanized, most city growth will continue to occur in developing countries. The pace of urbanization today in places such as Lagos and Bombay echoes that of Chicago and New York a century ago, but the absolute population increase is much higher. (See Table 2.) In just five years, between 1990 and 1995, the cities of the developing world grew by 263 million people—the equivalent of another Los Angeles or Shanghai forming every three months. Population increase in developing-country cities will continue to be the distinguishing demographic trend of the next century, accounting for nearly 90 percent of the 2.7 billion people projected by U.N. demographers (in their medium-growth scenario) to be

TABLE 1 (continued)

1900		2000	
	(million)		
London	6.5	Tokyo	28.0
New York	4.2	Mexico City	18.1
Paris	3.3	Bombay	18.0
Berlin	2.7	São Paulo	17.7
Chicago	1.7	New York	16.6
Vienna	1.7	Shanghai	14.2
Tokyo	1.5	Lagos	13.5
St. Petersburg	1.4	Los Angeles	13.1
Manchester	1.4	Seoul	12.9
Philadelphia	1.4	Beijing	12.4

Source: See endnote 15.

TABLE 2

Rate and Scale of Population Growth in Selected Industrial Cities, 1875–1900, and Developing Cities, 1975–2000

City	Annual Population Growth (percent)	Population Added (million)
Industrial Cities (1875–1900)		
Chicago	6.0	1.3
New York	3.3	2.3
Tokyo	2.6	0.7
London	1.7	2.2
Paris	1.6	1.1
Developing Cities (1975–2000)		
Lagos	5.8	10.2
Bombay	4.0	11.2
São Paolo	2.3	7.7
Mexico City	1.9	6.9
Shanghai	0.9	2.7

Source: See endnote 16.

added to world population between 1995 and 2030. (See Figure 1 and map.)[16]

As the view from outer space suggests, regional variations in urbanization within the Third World are striking. Some 73 percent of Latin Americans now live in cities, making the region roughly as urbanized as Europe and North America. The most explosive urban growth is expected in Africa and Asia, where only 30–35 percent of people live in cities now. In many parts of the developing world, particularly Southeast Asia and West Africa, urban numbers are hard to gauge because "circular" migrants—people who move to the city temporarily—elude census takers. In general, cities with more than 1 million people are often called "large," while membership in the "megacity" club generally requires a population of 10 million. By this definition, Africa has just

FIGURE 1

Urban Population in Industrial and Developing Regions, Selected Years

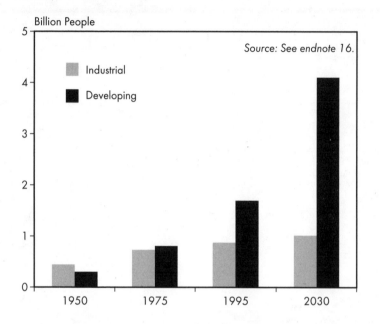

Source: See endnote 16.

one megacity, Lagos. But burgeoning African "mega-villages" of several hundred thousand are growing too fast for local authorities to manage. As urban numbers swell, cities present not only problems but also opportunities, as examples in the next sections will show.[17]

Closing the Water and Waste Circuits

Traditionally, human settlements have been sited to take advantage of water for agriculture and transportation. The world's earliest cities arose in the valleys of great rivers: the Nile, the Tigris-Euphrates, the Indus, and the Yellow. Rivers and streams that provide drinking water are also used

MAP

World's Largest Cities and Most Rapidly Urbanizing Countries, 1995

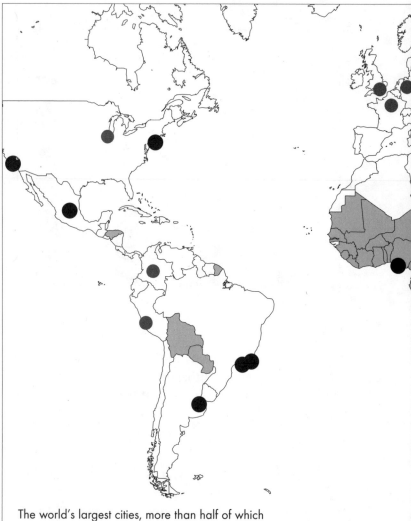

The world's largest cities, more than half of which are in Asia, are home to just 14 percent of the world's urban population. More people live in smaller cities and towns—and the fastest-growing ones are in Africa.

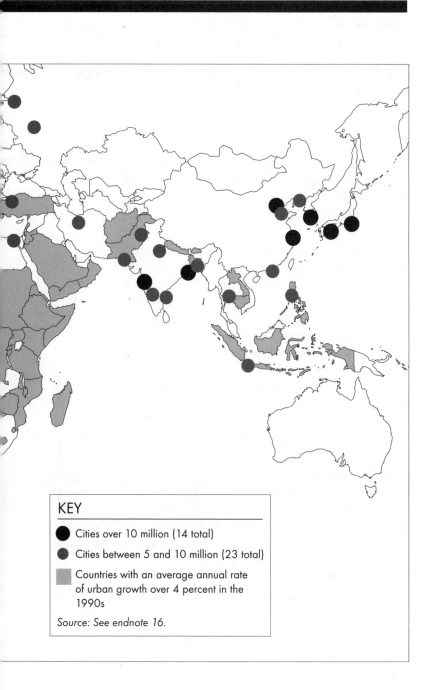

KEY

⬤ Cities over 10 million (14 total)

⬤ Cities between 5 and 10 million (23 total)

▢ Countries with an average annual rate of urban growth over 4 percent in the 1990s

Source: See endnote 16.

to carry household and industrial wastes away, so the flow of water into a city and the flow of wastes out are intimately linked. Of course, not all waste is borne by water. Remains from some of the earliest cities suggest that residents at first took a "devil-may-care" approach to solid waste disposal, simply raising the roofs of their houses as mounting garbage lifted street levels. In eighteenth-century Boston, when refuse in the streets threatened to impede the flow of traffic and the speed of commerce, the city's first "paved" roads were built: wooden planks placed on top of the garbage. A century later, Charles Dickens gave an idea of the water and waste problems of nineteenth-century New York when he described it as "a city without baths or plumbing, lighted by gas and scavenged by pigs."[18]

In order to minimize pollution, nineteenth-century engineers constructed vast water and sewer systems. The goal was twofold: to meet growing water demand by boosting supply, and to channel wastewater and rainwater away from people as quickly as possible. As anticipated, these systems were a great boon to health. With better water and sanitation, life expectancy in French cities, for instance, shot up from 32 years in 1850 to 45 years by 1900.[19]

But while large water and sanitation projects transformed city life in industrial countries, their benefits failed to reach much of the developing world. Despite gains during the 1980s, which were designated by the United Nations as the International Water Supply and Sanitation Decade, 25 percent of people in the developing world remain without clean water and 66 percent lack sanitation. Waterborne diarrheal diseases, which arise from poor water and waste management, are the world's leading cause of illness. Each year, 5 million children, mostly young and urban, perish from such ailments.[20]

Like waterborne waste, solid waste profoundly affects human health, and it too was a target for reformers in industrial cities of the nineteenth century. Today, such hazards are most pronounced in the developing world, where between one third and one half of city trash goes uncollected. In the 1950s, Manila began to dump much of its garbage in a poor neighborhood, laying the foundation for what would become a striking topographical feature—"Mount Smoky." Methane from the rotting refuse burned in an acrid haze, lending the summit its name. It towered 40 meters above sea level in Manila Bay until a newly elected Philippine president razed the garbage mountain in the early 1990s.[21]

Open piles of garbage attract disease-carrying rats and flies and often wash into drainage channels, where they contribute to floods and waterborne disease. And even the most expensive methods of waste disposal—high-tech "sanitary" landfills and incinerators—are not completely free of health risks. Toxins from landfills can leach into groundwater, and heavy metals, chlorine compounds, and dioxin are among the hazardous components of incinerator ash.[22]

Moreover, water and waste technologies designed to promote health often contribute to broader environmental ills. The first class of water-related problems arises in bringing water into cities. The architect Vitruvius wrote in the first century B.C. that finding water was the first step in planning a new city. But city builders today assume that having water close by is not very important as they can rely on engineers to divert rivers or pump water over great distances. Thus, cities have extended their reach for water to faraway places, destroying fragile ecosystems. When rivers are diverted and dammed to serve thirsty cities, their natural functions suffer. A study of the largest river systems in the United States, Canada, Europe, and the former Soviet Union found that diversions imperiled waterfalls, rapids, and floodplain wetlands—all important habitats for a diversity of plant and animal species.[23]

To irrigate their crops, farmers take some 65 percent of all the water people use, but they are facing more competition for this life-giving resource than ever before. Since the turn of the century, combined municipal and industrial use of water worldwide has grown 24 times, while agricultural use has increased only 5 times. Researchers at the International Food Policy Research Institute estimate that if cities in the developing world grow as projected, the share of water going to households and industries will more than double, from 13 percent of total water use to 27 percent. As water analyst Sandra Postel notes, "Just two decades ago, serious water problems were confined to manageable pockets of the world. Today, however, they exist on every continent and are spreading rapidly." Prime examples of water problems exacerbated by urban growth include the western United States—where water battles are being waged between farmers and urbanites—and northern China, where 108 cities report shortages, and farmers are losing water not only to cities and industry, but also to their toxic discharges. Some 80 percent of China's major rivers are so polluted that fish can no longer live in them.[24]

Just as diverting water to cities can cause problems, so, too, can rushing it away through pipes and gutters. When rainwater is channeled into sewers, less water infiltrates the soil to recharge underground supplies. Roads also prevent water from seeping into the ground. Thus rain runs off pavement straight into channels, where it speeds into rivers and streams, causing more severe floods than would occur if plants and soil soaked up some of the deluge. Moreover, without enough water to recharge underground supplies, the land above may subside. Subsidence is exacerbated when aquifers are overpumped. The sinking land can cause rail tracks to buckle, water pipes to burst, and building foundations to crack. In coastal areas, saltwater may leak into wells, ruining drinking supplies.[25]

A dramatic image of subsidence appears in a 1995 report on Mexico City's water supply. At first, the photo of a small boy leaning against what appears to be a telephone pole looks out of place in a book about water. But the pole is actually a well casing that was once underground. Excessive withdrawal of groundwater has caused parts of Mexico City to sink more than 9 meters in the last century, so now the pipe towers some 7 meters above ground. Local children reportedly mark their height on it to see if they grow faster than the ground sinks.[26]

Much as storm drains short-circuit the water cycle, urban waste disposal systems designed to move wastes away from people interrupt the nutrient cycle. Trucks, planes, and trains haul food into cities from great distances, but the nutrients rarely make it back to farmland. The U.N. Food and Agricultural Organization (FAO) estimates that a city of about 10 million people in the developing world—Cairo or Rio, for instance—brings in at least 6,000 tons of food per day. New York, with 16 million inhabitants, imports 20,000 tons. Roughly half of this food is transformed into human energy; the other half is shunted to sewers or trucked to increasingly remote landfills. Ironically, preventing the normal return of organic waste to the soil where it originated adds to the waste disposal burden in cities, while heightening the demand among farmers for manufactured fertilizer. Excess nitrogen from industrial fertilizer is a growing threat to ecological health. Plants adapted to excess nitrogen thrive at the expense of other species, speeding the loss of certain plants and animals on land. Further, soils in many regions are now so saturated with nitrogen that nitrates are carrying away vital nutrients such as calcium and potassium into streams or groundwater. Overenrichment of estuaries and coastal waters with nitrogen is thought to be at least partly responsible for the surge in toxic algal blooms that killed huge numbers of fish and shellfish around the world in the 1980s.[27]

A key to water conservation is removing incentives for prolifigate use.

Moreover, throwing away items instead of reusing or recycling them increases the demand for new resources obtained by environmentally destructive mining and logging. In 1895, George Waring, New York City's commissioner of street cleaning, recognized that the "out of sight, out of mind" approach to trash disposal "is an easy one to follow, but it is not an economical one, nor a decent one, nor a safe one." But his prescient warning went unheeded. In the industrial world, waste collection has improved public health, but the problem of waste generation has only worsened. New York's own trash mountain on Staten Island, the Fresh Kills landfill, is better maintained than Manila's Mount Smoky was, but it is far larger, spreading across 1,214 hectares and rising 53 meters—higher than New York's 47-meter Statue of Liberty. Urbanites in industrial countries generate up to 100 times more refuse per person than their counterparts in developing countries.[28]

Of necessity, water-short and waste-filled cities of the next century will be pressed to slake their thirst and dispose of their waste in ways that cause less ecological destruction and require less money. Among their options are land use restrictions that protect water at its source and conservation strategies that make the most of the water that reaches the city. (While a world energy crisis in the 1970s prompted people to begin to think seriously about reducing demand, water has yet to become a major target for efficiency gains.) Other approaches include low-cost methods of wastewater treatment. Cities also have the potential to shift from being repositories of waste to becoming important sources of raw materials. To some extent, the forests and mines of the twenty-first century may well be found in our urban centers—in the form of city recycling plants. Local authorities can spur the transition by providing incentives for composting, recycling, and waste-based industries.

Conservation of land protects water quality. A number of cities are finding that cooperating with neighboring regions, industries, and agriculture to protect watersheds is ultimately less costly than trying to make polluted water safe for drinking. New York City, for instance, plans to buy $300 million worth of land upstate to protect the watersheds that harbor the city's drinking water. The tactic is part of a comprehensive watershed protection strategy that, while costly at $1.4 billion, will save the city from having to pay $3–$8 billion for a new filtration system. In Costa Rica, the city of San José has recently embarked on a plan to clean up and protect its water. Waste dumped in the Rio Torres has endangered public health and marine life. The city has set up a watershed agency, the first of its kind in Central America, to help implement the plan to better manage the resource.[29]

Limiting development near important water sources not only preserves water quality, it also prevents floods and provides a connection to nature. In the 1880s, landscape architect Frederick Law Olmsted persuaded Boston that keeping buildings away from floodplains by establishing riverfront parks would ultimately prove cheaper than keeping floods away from buildings through huge public works projects. The result was the verdant Back Bay Fens, a park that protected the neighborhood from flooding.[30]

In this century, metropolitan Boston has provided an example of successful water conservation. Since 1987, the Massachusetts Water Resources Authority has managed to avoid diverting two large rivers to augment supply, as engineers had initially prescribed. Instead, for a third to half the cost of the diversions, the government has reduced total water demand 24 percent by repairing leaky pipes, installing water-saving fixtures, and teaching everyone from school-children to plant managers how to save water.[31]

Water conservation is not only for rich nations; developing countries also stand to save considerable amounts of money by reining in wastage. In the Third World, as much as 70 percent of water is lost through leaky pipes and theft. In Manila, for example, 58 percent of the drinking water is forfeited to leaks or illegal tapping, while Singapore, where pipes are better maintained, loses only 8 percent.[32]

A key to water conservation is removing incentives for profligate use. Lack of meters, inordinately low prices, and prices that decline as use increases all encourage wastefulness. Water is underpriced because a higher level of government limits the amount that a utility can charge. And subsidies allow water companies to charge less than needed to recover costs. This underpricing rewards excessive use, so the problem feeds on itself. With the cash-strapped water agency unable to maintain its pipes, more water is lost to leaks. The loss prompts the agency to lay claim to additional water supplies, diverting them from agriculture. And as farms fail without irrigation, more people migrate to cities, raising the demand for water. Bogor, Indonesia, took its first steps to break this cycle in 1988, when it installed meters and hiked prices to encourage households to conserve. Demand initially fell by one third, allowing the utility to connect more families to the system without increasing the amount of water used.[33]

Although pricing the poor out of water is a concern, artificially low prices may hurt this group even more than high ones would. Prices that do not reflect the true cost of water discourage utilities from extending service—it would be a losing proposition. Thus many of the poor in developing countries end up paying much more for water from private vendors, who charge anywhere from four to 100 times the public rate. In Istanbul, water from vendors is 10 times the public rate; in Bombay, it is 20 times higher. Meanwhile, wealthy citizens get to pay the lower fee.[34]

Another conservation technique, making better use of rainwater, has the added advantage of doubling as a flood-control strategy. Metropolitan Tokyo, with 82 percent of its land surface covered by asphalt or concrete, suffers from torrential runoff that causes floods and fails to replenish underground water supplies. In response, the city has turned to rainwater as a supplemental source, thereby both cutting back demand on aquifers and reducing flooding. Tanks atop 579 city buildings now capture this free resource for use in washrooms, gardens, air-conditioning systems, and fire hoses. Rain that falls on the giant Kokugikan sumo wrestling stadium, for instance, supplies 70 percent of the water in the building that is not used for drinking.[35]

Other forms of water recycling also hold potential to enhance city water supplies. Municipal wastewater can be used instead of high-quality drinking water to flush toilets or to water lawns. If treated, it may be used to irrigate some types of crops or to raise fish—some 70 percent of Israeli wastewater is recycled in this way. Yet most urban water supply systems inhibit recycling. The bulk of the water that is

collected and treated to drinking water standards is ultimately used to flush toilets, and then joins the city's wastewater stream. "Since wastewater collection, treatment, and
disposal is typically twice as expensive as providing water in
the first place," notes Harvard's Peter Rogers, "it is truly sur-
prising that little has been done to question the wisdom of
the conventional systems." Treatment can be made easier
and cheaper if wastewater from industry is kept separate
from the residential flow. In most countries, the flows are
combined, however. Cities in developing
countries could leapfrog over this problem when they build sewage infrastructure by keeping flows separate and using
lower-quality water to flush toilets, thus
saving money and water.[36]

**The forests and
mines of the
twenty-first
century may
well be found
in our urban
centers.**

In addition to improving water supply and quality, cities can also treat
wastewater at lower economic and environmental cost. One approach—wetlands treatment—uses more land than
conventional treatment plants but is
much less expensive and does not produce toxic sludge.
Vegetation in stabilization ponds or modified wetlands
extracts contaminants such as nitrates and mercury, while
bacteria and other organisms break down these toxic compounds. Phoenix, Arizona, is creating wetlands to clean a
portion of its sewage because this option is much cheaper
than a $625-million upgrade of its wastewater treatment
plant would be.[37]

Organic waste—paper, food scraps, lawn clippings, and
even human waste—is a valuable resource. In industrial
countries, food and yard waste alone accounts for some 36
percent of the municipal waste stream. European cities are
leading a trend toward composting, which transforms this
castoff organic matter into a product that invigorates agricultural soils. Cities in seven countries—Austria, Belgium,
Denmark, Germany, Luxembourg, the Netherlands, and
Switzerland—recover more than 85 percent of these wastes.[38]

To keep paper and inorganic materials such as metals, glass, and plastics from landfills, a number of cities have found ways to promote recycling and waste-based industries. They can charge a fee for the collection of unsorted garbage, for example, while picking up at no cost refuse that has been separated for recycling. By adopting "pay-as-you-throw" systems, at least 11 U.S. cities have boosted recycling rates to the 45–60 percent range, well above the national average of 27 percent.[39]

Some cities have gone a step further toward preventing landfill overflow by involving the industries that create disposable goods or generate waste. In 1997, Tokyo municipal officials looking for new waste disposal options in land-short Japan announced that they would require makers and distributors of plastic bottles to recover and recycle their products. And Graz, Austria, has created a labeling program to spur small- and medium-sized industries to reduce waste: companies receive the city's Ecoprofit label if they reduce solid waste by 30 percent and hazardous waste by 50 percent.[40]

A handful of cities are even moving beyond recycling to "industrial symbiosis," where one company's waste becomes another's input. The first eco-industrial park began to evolve more than 20 years ago in Kalundborg, Denmark. Today, waste gases from an oil refinery there are burned by a power plant, waste heat from the plant warms commercial fish ponds, and other companies use byproducts of combustion to make wallboard and concrete. According to one calculation, Kalundborg's waste-saving approach translates into $120 million in savings and revenues on a $60-million investment over a five-year period.[41]

Since 1993, more than 20 U.S. cities hoping to revive stagnant economies have announced plans for parks similar to Kalundborg's. Chattanooga, Tennessee's proposed SMART Park is one of the most imaginative. Now a leader in environmental technologies such as recycling and electric buses, Chattanooga has transformed itself from the most polluted city in America to one of the most livable in less than three decades. Its zero-waste park, which would include factories,

retail stores, and residences, would expand the city's meta-
morphosis. Underground tunnels would link some 30 buildings, 10 of which exist already, to share heating, cooling,
wastes, and industrial water supplies. For instance, excess
heat generated by existing foundries would be used to warm
water at a nearby chicken-processing plant. Biomass waste
from this factory would be turned into energy at a new
ethanol facility. And nutrient byproducts from the ethanol
plant could be used to support a greenhouse, a tree nursery,
and a fish farm.[42]

City partnerships with local nongovernmental organizations (NGOs) and private business can promote innovations in water supply, sanitation, waste collection, and
recycling. Where cities have been unable or unwilling to
extend water and waste services to their poorest inhabitants,
some neighborhoods have stepped into the breach with low-
cost solutions. One of the most successful examples is in the
Orangi district of Karachi, Pakistan, home to nearly 1 million
"squatters." In the early 1980s, Akhter Hameed Khan, a
dynamic community organizer, formed an NGO called the
Orangi Pilot Project. Between 1981 and 1996, this group
helped neighborhoods to organize, collect money, and manage construction of sewers that now serve some 90 percent of
Orangi's residents.[43]

The decentralized approach exemplified by the Orangi
district can also work with solid waste. Local authorities
have struck recycling deals with self-employed wastepickers
in several cities in the developing world. In Cairo, the
Zabbaleen people have been garbage pickers since they began
coming to Cairo in mid-century. With the help of aid agencies, the city and the community launched a program in
1981 to improve city collection service and boost the
Zabbaleen's income and standard of living. Today, the
Zabbaleen sew rags into quilts and compost animal waste to
sell to farmers. Similarly, city officials in Bandung, Indonesia,
are now working with a local NGO to employ a group of
scavenger families. The families receive financial and technical support to separate recyclables more safely and efficient-

ly than they now do, to compost organic wastes, and to create businesses that use the wastes they collect as raw materials. They make money—and the city reduces the cost of waste management.[44]

The job creation potential of recycling may be even greater in more wasteful societies. Studies in the United States, for example, have found recycling generates many more local jobs than landfilling or incinerating waste does. In New York City's South Bronx, two nonprofit groups—the Natural Resources Defense Council and the Banana Kelly community association—have teamed up to build a mill that will use municipal wastewater to recycle 400,000 tons of the city's wastepaper into 330,000 tons of newsprint each year. The mill is expected to create 400 permanent local jobs and $30 million in annual tax revenue.[45]

Increasingly, cities are looking to tap the resources of the private sector. While the private sector has a long history in solid waste collection and disposal, it is just entering water supply and sanitation because governments realize that they will be unable to come up with the billions of dollars needed over the next decade for reliable water systems. A team of researchers in the United States has calculated that $1 trillion a year—a fourfold increase over current spending—would be needed to supply developing countries with conventional water supply and sanitation technologies by 2020.[46]

Water privatization is most extensive in the United Kingdom and France, and companies from these countries are beginning to ply their trade abroad. Only 5 percent of the financing for water worldwide comes from private sources, but privatization, in various degrees, is a growing trend. Between 1990 and 1997, the number of private water projects in developing countries increased more than 10-fold, mainly in Latin America and East Asia. In Buenos Aires, for instance, an international consortium led by the French firm Lyonnaise des Eaux-Dumez renovated thousands of kilometers of pipes in the water system, and was thereby able to expand coverage and lower rates at the same time.[47]

Still, privatization is not a panacea. Water supply and sanitation are important public services, so some form of public control or regulation will always be needed to make sure that quality and prices are reasonable. Investors may find providing water more attractive than taking it away—the cost invested in water supply can be recovered by user fees, whereas it is harder to charge for sewers each time they are used—but both services are essential to the common welfare. Few cities have regulations in place yet to make privatization work equitably.[48]

Toward Greater Self-Reliance in Food and Energy

Food and energy have shaped urban history. Residents of Aztec, Mayan, and Incan cities built earthworks and water delivery systems to grow food for human and animal use and to produce wood for fuel. High-intensity farming was a hallmark of early civilizations on Java and in the Indus Valley. Most historical analysis suggests that agriculture made cities possible, as increased crop yields could support larger populations. Attempting to overturn conventional wisdom, urban critic Jane Jacobs argues that cities made rural agriculture possible. Jacobs reasons that agricultural techniques were simply the first of numerous technologies that cities created and then exported to their hinterlands. Either way, growth in agriculture is clearly linked to the growth of cities.[49]

The pace at which cities grew was also greatly influenced by changes in energy technologies. Before the Industrial Revolution, when wind, water, wood, human, and animal power fueled cities, their populations remained below 1 million. With the advent of coal and steam engines, however, gigantic urban factories became feasible. And if coal and steam concentrated populations in the industrial cities of the eighteenth and nineteenth centuries, the rise of the petroleum-fueled automobile allowed twentieth-century cities to spread far beyond their dense urban cores.[50]

Long supply lines for food and fuels may have doomed some early civilizations. Ancient Rome is a case in point. During the time of Caesar, Romans settled North Africa, cleared the forests, used the logs for timber and fuel, and began to farm the deforested land—transforming it into the breadbasket of the Roman Empire. According to British writer Herbert Girardet, by the year 100 A.D., up to 500,000 tons of grain were being shipped from Africa to Rome annually, and the nutrients from that food never returned to replenish African soils. Loss of soil fertility and deforestation in Northern Africa, according to Girardet, contributed to the decline of Rome by undermining its food supply.[51]

Twentieth-century transportation systems have stretched food and energy supply lines to new lengths, as production has become ever larger and more centralized. Agricultural research has focused on industrial farms, plantations, and commercial grain crops. Huge chain supermarkets are now the dominant food outlets in industrial countries: some 75 percent of food in the United Kingdom is sold through such stores. Similarly, the plants that generate electrical power have become enormous: the average size of a new turbine generator built in the United States increased from 10 megawatts in 1910 to around 600 megawatts by the early 1990s.[52]

Although these large systems excel at producing more food and electricity with fewer employees, they are also highly energy consuming and polluting and require complex distribution routes, with use occurring far from the site of generation. Before reaching the table, food may now go through numerous steps: assembling, handling, processing, packaging, transport, storage, wholesaling, and retailing. Germany's Wuppertal Institute found that the ingredients and packaging components in a jar of strawberry yogurt had to travel 3,494 kilometers before reaching a supermarket. Attenuated supply lines mean that hikes in food or fuel prices, transport strikes, and natural disasters can jeopardize urban food security. Likewise, electric grid systems depend on large power plants and long transmission lines, which makes them vulnerable to various kinds of breakdown. Nevertheless, both food and energy systems are fairly reliable in industrial countries, but not in developing countries.[53]

Moreover, industrial agriculture and energy systems have damaged the environment. Corporations in the industrial world have centralized seed supply, providing farmers with a few highly marketable varieties. These species are carefully selected—sometimes even genetically engineered—to boost yields. As a result, crops have become genetically uniform, and more vulnerable to attack from constantly evolving plant and insect enemies. Moreover, the pesticides and industrial fertilizers needed to sustain these crops threaten human health and pollute the water. In the energy sector, mining for coal and uranium is ecologically devastating. Nitrogen and sulfur from coal combustion acidify lakes, forests, and farms, and carbon contributes to global climate change. And despite gains in productivity, some 828 million people remain hungry in the developing world, and roughly 2 billion lack electricity.[54]

800 million urban farmers today harvest 15 percent of the world's food supply.

With a combination of techniques, old and new, cities can develop greater self-reliance in food and energy, close the nutrient loop, and reduce the fuels they require. Homegrown food and clean, locally produced energy can not only green a city, but also increase income and security for its inhabitants.

Farms that are close to people are less likely to rely on chemical fertilizers and pesticides, as neighbors have a vested interest in non-toxic production. Community-supported agriculture, which took root in Japan, Switzerland, and Germany in the 1960s and 1970s, is one way in which urban dwellers in industrial countries are beginning to connect with small farmers in nearby agricultural areas. Consumers pay a farmer a fee at the beginning of the growing season in exchange for a box of vegetables each week. Since the 1980s, some 1,000 such operations have sprouted in 43 U.S. states, where the farthest reaches of suburbia are often situated on prime growing soil. Farmers who are engulfed by expanding metropolitan areas often adapt to higher land values by farming their land more intensively. The dollar value of agricultural production from within U.S. metropolitan areas increased from 30 percent in 1980 to 40 percent in 1990.[55]

More food can be grown around cities—and fostered by community-supported agriculture programs—than directly within them. Nevertheless, the potential for agriculture inside the city is substantial. Urban farming includes vegetables grown on roofs and patios, market gardens on vacant plots, and fish harvested from tanks or sewage lagoons. In the first global survey of urban agriculture, the U.N. Development Programme (UNDP) estimates that 800 million urban farmers today harvest 15 percent of the world's food supply. The potential is much greater.[56]

Urban agriculture has a long history in Asia. As Franklin King recounts in *Farmers of Forty Centuries*, Chinese cities have long protected their surrounding areas for agriculture and preserved their city wastes to apply on fields. Even into the 1980s, urban farmers in China's 18 largest cities met over 90 percent of their cities' vegetable demand and over half of their meat and poultry demand. However, these numbers are likely lower now due to intensive building. With protective measures, even dense little urban islands can raise much of their own food: Hong Kong produces two thirds of the poultry and close to half of the vegetables it consumes, and Singapore, which licenses nearly 10,000 farmers, is self-sufficient in meat and produces one fourth of its own vegetables.[57]

Urban farming is significant in a few other regions. In parts of Africa, urban agriculture is truly a survival strategy for poor residents. Some 68 percent of families in Dar es Salaam, Tanzania, grow vegetables or raise livestock, and as much as 70 percent of all poultry in Kampala, Uganda, is raised in the city. And in Europe, the green movement is spurring a resurgence of city farming, a popular practice in the 19th century. From the 1850s through the early 1900s, intensive horticulture covered one sixth of the area of Paris. The crops, sustained by manure from the city's horse stables, produced a surplus of fresh vegetables that were exported. Today, the legatees of this urban tradition are reviving it primarily for the sake of the environment. One of the nations leading the rebirth of urban agriculture on the European continent is the Netherlands, which is densely populated yet maintains a vibrant green core between its major cities. In Germany, 80,000 Berliners tend community gardens, and another 16,000 are on waiting lists.[58]

Small farms in and around cities often face daunting obstacles. They may find it hard to compete with industrial farms, which benefit from economies of scale. If direct crop subsidies and hidden energy subsidies to mega-farms were eliminated, however, local farms might gain a competitive edge. Small farms do have important advantages. Although they spend more money on labor, they save in other areas. For example, organic growing methods reduce the need for expensive pesticides and fertilizers, and local distribution lowers the cost of marketing, storage, and transport.[59]

In cities, laws often limit or prohibit growing crops or raising animals because agriculture is not seen as a profitable or an aesthetically pleasing use of expensive urban land. Yet some types of urban agriculture, such as gardens on rooftops and balconies, do not require a plot of ground. Moreover, there are usually places for short-term gardens in vacant lots, and for long-term farming in parkland, floodplains, and steep slopes and wetlands that are not safe for building. City planners could steer would-be farmers to these areas, as greenery can actually enhance vacant lots and help prevent flooding and soil erosion along floodplains and slopes.[60]

The most serious objection to urban agriculture is its potential threat to public health. But rather than eliminate urban farming in order to solve this problem, cities could promote and require safe practices by supplying compost and treated sewage, and by mandating organic farming methods to alleviate the need for chemical fertilizers and pesticides that contaminate water and air. Cities can look to groups such as FAO and the World Health Organization (WHO) for standards and procedures for using wastewater and solid waste in farming. In order to protect crops from urban pollution, buffer trees can be placed between them and the road. In highly polluted areas near roads and factories, farmers can plant root crops and fruit trees rather than green, leafy vegetables, which are more susceptible to heavy metal contamination.[61]

The rewards of greater self-reliance in food are wide ranging. City farms and gardens can be nourished with urban organic waste and wastewater, thereby reducing the problems and costs of waste management. For instance, aquatic plants such as duckweed and water hyacinth that are grown in sewage lagoons provide two benefits: a food crop for livestock and purified water. Curitiba, Brazil, has devised a unique way to promote sanitation while boosting nutrition. Since 1991, the city has taken the money it would otherwise pay waste collectors to fetch garbage from hard-to-reach slums, and has spent it on food from local farms. For every bag of waste brought to a waste collection site, a low-income family gets a bag of locally grown vegetables and fruits.[62]

Moreover, small food businesses provide jobs, boosting the local economy. As population surges in cities, urban agriculture stands to provide needed nutrition. Agriculture provides the highest self-employment earnings in small-scale enterprises in Nairobi, and the third highest in all of urban Kenya. Urban farms can serve as a source of both environmental education and employment for young people, whereas corporate agriculture pulls money out of a community. The European Federation of City Farms, founded in 1990, represents 1,000 projects that focus on education in eight countries. Among urban food projects in the United States are a youth-run system of farms and markets that generates $1 million in annual sales and employs teenagers in inner-city Boston, and a half-acre organic market garden in San Francisco that offers jobs and hope to former prison inmates.[63]

Greater self-reliance in energy, also, is possible with

promising new decentralized energy technologies. Solar electric panels, for instance, can be mounted atop urban roofs. The newest technologies can even be integrated into standard building materials such as roofing shingles, tiles, and window glass—turning the building surface into a nearly invisible power generator. While solar electricity has long been economical in remote areas, the 1990s have seen thousands of solar panels hoisted atop homes and office buildings in industrial-country cities such as Tokyo, Berlin, and Zurich—places that are already well served by an electrical grid. Since 1993, a locally owned electric utility in California, the Sacramento Municipal Utility District (SMUD), has installed grid-linked solar panels on more than 420 homes and buildings and above several parking lots. According to the utility, the city could generate at least one sixth of the local peak demand by covering available south-to-west-facing roofs, parking lots, and transmission corridors with solar panels. Geothermal heat pumps that move heat from the ground to a building in cold weather, and from the building to the ground in warm weather are also growing in popularity. Small natural gas turbines that generate both heat and electricity are another option.[64]

Cogeneration with an older and centralized technology, district heating, already saves considerable energy in northern European cities. In conventional power plants, more than half of the energy is wasted; with district heating systems, excess heat from electricity generation warms water that is piped to buildings throughout the city. In Copenhagen, district heating meets 67 percent of the space heating demands, and expansions under way will enable it to supply fully 95 percent by 2002.[65]

Energy efficient buildings, designed for the local climate, can complement locally produced solar power and district heating. In the town of Kemalpasa, Turkey, traditional underground or semi-buried homes take advantage of the Earth's natural heating and cooling—and as a result use at least 75 percent less energy than new houses. Homes in a Davis, California, subdivision, sited to capture sunlight only at certain times of the day and year, use nearly 60 percent less energy than comparable area residences. The National Renewable Energy Laboratory estimates that such climate-sensitive design could cut energy use for heating and cooling in U.S. homes by 70 percent on average, yielding tremendous savings. An energy code for buildings adopted in 1978 in California had saved $11.4 billion by 1995. Toronto, Canada, which has teamed up with energy service companies and financial institutions to retrofit 1 percent of the city's buildings, anticipates $900,000 annual savings in energy costs, which will go to future investments in energy efficiency.[66]

Landscaping around a building helps determine how much energy its residents will need for heating and cooling. The United States Forest Service estimated that planting 95,000 trees in metropolitan Chicago would result in net savings of $38 million over a 30-year period in avoided energy use and other environmental benefits. Vegetation can also be planted directly on buildings for this purpose. Ecological roof gardens planted with native grasses are becoming fairly commonplace in Germany and the Netherlands. Unlike traditional roof gardens that require maintenance, these typically need little or no irrigation or fertilizer. In Malaysia, a 15-story skyscraper is covered with tropical plants that cool the building naturally, thus reducing energy needs.[67]

A combination of old and new technologies enabled the city of Saarbrucken in Germany's coal-rich Saar Valley to reduce per capita carbon emissions from coal burning by 16 percent between 1990 and 1996. Saarbrucken achieved this feat with efficiency gains in buildings, expansion of its district heating system, and solar electric panels placed strategically on rooftops.[68]

Decentralized energy, like urban agriculture, must overcome barriers. Most utilities discourage small power producers and do not let them connect to the grid. Efforts under way in some countries to standardize such interconnections will help. And the restructuring of electric power markets that is now sweeping the globe may open up new opportunities. Now available in Japan, Switzerland, and half of the

U.S. states is a key financial incentive to level the playing field for solar power, "net metering," in which electric companies purchase electricity produced by individual solar rooftops at the same price they charge consumers. To boost its solar supply between 1998 and 2002, Sacramento's electric utility has begun to sell grid-connected solar electric systems to interested homeowners, and to buy back the electricity produced by their roofs. Consumers and the utility alike benefit. Consumers can take electricity from the utility's grid at night and on cloudy days, so they do not have to invest in batteries to store the sun's energy. And the utility gains an extra generating source that is strongest on sunny afternoons—just when electricity is in high demand for air conditioning.[69]

There are many advantages to greater self-reliance in energy. Trees, whether planted for agriculture or to reduce the energy needs of buildings, have other environmental benefits: absorbing air pollution, cooling streets, and reducing runoff. A software program distributed by the Washington, DC-based NGO American Forests calculates the amount of money that trees save a city by shading buildings or blocking them from the wind, sucking up stormwater, and filtering the air. It found, for instance, that Milwaukee's trees spare the city an estimated $305 million by absorbing stormwater runoff, rendering the construction of additional dams, dikes, and levies unnecessary. Trees also provide a connection with nature often missing in the built environment. A study published in *Science* documented a psychological effect of greener cities: patients with a view of a park from their hospital window fared better than those with a view of a wall.[70]

Local energy production and energy efficiency businesses also have the potential to invigorate city economies. According to analysis by David Morris at the Institute for Local Self-Reliance, money spent on energy tends to remain in the local economy for less time than money used for food or other items. Studies in two U.S. cities found that only 15 cents of each dollar spent on energy returned to benefit the local economy.[71]

As densely populated pieces of land, cities are limited in their ability to produce their own food and energy. Yet rooftop gardening and building-scale power generation are among the many practices and technologies that could substantially boost local production—and offer wide-ranging benefits to the local environment and economy.

Linking Transportation and Land Use

Changes in urban water, waste, food, and energy ultimately hinge on the transportation and land use decisions that shape cities. By building roads, rail lines, or bike paths, cities determine not only how people will move around, but also where the accessible and desirable buildings will be. And by mandating where new buildings can be built and what kind of uses—residential, retail, industrial—are allowed, land use and zoning laws influence how far people must travel to get to work, buy food, and go about their daily business, and how much land is paved over. Taken together, transportation and land use decisions influence where new water, waste, and energy services will be needed, and to what extent urban development will erase farmland. To create better places to live without threatening the planet, local authorities can augment sensible planning with financial incentives and partnerships with the private sector.[72]

While walking distances constrained life in the earliest cities, by the end of the nineteenth century, electric trolley and rail tracks stretched growing industrial cities into radial spokes. Early twentieth-century "streetcar suburbs" in North America and Europe were initially compact, with houses a short walk from the stations. Next, the automobile allowed the city to spread out in a more random fashion than ever before—a trend the United States was quickest to adopt. By the 1930s, developers were building houses and roads between the rail lines for people with cars.[73]

Responding to pollution and overcrowding in the late

nineteenth and early twentieth centuries, reformers sketched idealized images of transportation and land use for the future. Among the most influential visionaries was Ebenezer Howard, a British stenographer-turned-reformer. "Ill-ventilated, unplanned, unwieldy, and unhealthy" cities, Howard declared in 1902, had no place in a more humane future. Instead, a new network of clean, self-sufficient "garden cities" would marry the best social aspects of city life to the beauty of nature. French architect Le Corbusier, a generation after Howard, was also offended by the industrial cities of his time: "They are ineffectual, they use up our bodies, they thwart our souls." Le Corbusier envisioned gleaming skyscrapers surrounded by parks and wide motorways that would shape a "radiant city" worthy of the new century.[74]

Stand in any city today and you will see some of the forms prescribed by Howard and Le Corbusier. But you will not see the outcome these visionaries intended: a more equitable society in harmony with nature. Chaotic suburban development in the United States, for instance, is a caricature of Howard's garden city ideal. A sketch of "A Contemporary City" in Le Corbusier's 1924 book *L'Urbanisme* shows "one of the main tracks for fast motor traffic" nearly devoid of cars and bordered by tall buildings "bathed in light and air." Today, the traffic that clogs such roads darkens the sky and pollutes the air. Towering office blocks, Le Corbusier's "islands in the sky," were supposed to allow more room for nature below. But when it came to executing these attractive plans, the space for nature shrank.[75]

Australian researchers Peter Newman and Jeff Kenworthy have documented escalating car use in the United States as part of a larger study of transportation between 1970 and 1990 in 47 major metropolitan areas in Asia, Australia, Europe, and North America. On average, each person in the U.S. cities sampled in 1990 drove 10,870 kilometers (6,750 miles) within the metropolitan area, a distance greater than a round trip across the North American continent. Growth in car use in the U.S. cities between 1980 in 1990 was 2,000 kilometers per person, nearly double the increase in the Canadian cities, which have the next-highest driving level.[76] (See Figure 2.)

Suburban roads and houses supplant more than 1 million hectares of farmland each year in the United States, much of it on prime agricultural soil. The satellite map of nighttime lights for the United States corresponds well to census estimates of the nation's urban area. In a recent study, researchers comparing the lit area covered by cities to FAO's digital soil map found that while only 3 percent of the United States land surface is urbanized, the best soils are being paved over first. For instance, in California and Illinois, the top states for agricultural production, the proportion of the best soils occupied by urban areas is far greater than the share of

FIGURE 2

Annual Per Capita Car Use in Selected Cities, by Regional Average, 1970–90[1]

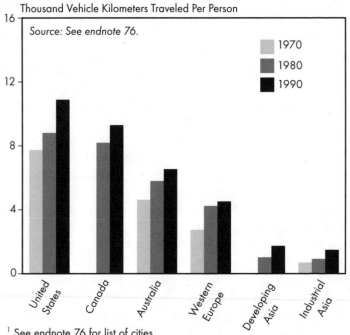

Thousand Vehicle Kilometers Traveled Per Person

Source: See endnote 76.

1970
1980
1990

[1] See endnote 76 for list of cities.

total land area covered by cities.[77]

Not surprisingly, some developing countries are emulating the U.S. model. According to government estimates, some 200,000 hectares of arable land in China disappear each year under city streets and developments. In Thailand as recently as 1959, a group of U.S. consultants noted: "To a person accustomed to Western standards, [Bangkok] is remarkable for its compactness. A vigorous walker can traverse it from north to south in three hours or less." But as population soared and this city built for canal traffic became dominated by motorized vehicles, Bangkok's built-up area mushroomed from 67 square kilometers in 1953 to 426 square kilometers in 1990. Today, even the most vigorous walker would probably not contemplate a transcity trip on foot; in fact, it can take three hours to cross Bangkok by car.[78]

Both the arrangement of buildings and ease of access to them help determine the livability of a city. Streets come alive with pedestrians when shops, factories, offices, and houses are all within walking distance of each other. And city greenery and parks between buildings cool streets and soothe the spirit. In contrast, public life diminishes when architects design office parks and shopping malls to be enjoyed from the inside only, surrounding them with gaping parking lots that welcome cars but not pedestrians. Crime often plagues fragmented cities, which isolate the poor in distinct pockets. Brazilian scholar Raquel Rolnick has exposed the link between territorial exclusion and violence in cities within the state of São Paulo. And urban analyst Jane Jacobs has noted the reverse relationship: a diverse street life usually means peace and security. Studying Manhattan, Jacobs concluded that many "eyes on the street" deter crime.[79]

Car-centered transportation systems not only erode street life but also promote social inequity. One third of the U.S. population are too young, too old, or too poor to drive. When private cars are the only viable means of transportation, these people are stranded. Some 98 percent of Boston's welfare recipients live within walking distance of public transit, but only 32 percent of potential employers are that close to a transit station. In the developing world, as much as 80 percent of the population can afford a bicycle, but only 5–10 percent earn enough to buy a car.[80]

Sprawling conurbations also threaten human health. Roads designed to make it easier for vehicles to go fast are often dangerous to people. Worldwide, traffic accidents kill some 885,000 people each year—equivalent to 10 fatal jumbo jet crashes per day—and injure many times this number. Fatal crashes tend to increase with greater numbers of cars and car trips. The exception is cities in developing countries, where low car use is offset by poor traffic signals and safety regulations. Nonetheless, researchers Newman and Kenworthy found that car use is so high in the U.S. metropolises they examined that in per capita traffic fatalities these cities exceed even the developing Asian cities they sampled. (See Table 3.)[81]

Vehicle exhaust is often the dominant ingredient in urban air pollution, which takes at least 3 million lives worldwide each year. Traffic pollution is increasingly smothering developing cities, particularly in Asia and Latin America. Vehicles contribute an estimated 60–70 percent of key urban air pollutants in Central America and 50–60 percent in India. In 1995, ozone levels in Mexico City exceeded the national standard on 324 days; during the same year, the hourly standard in Santiago, Chile, was surpassed 404 times. Another air pollutant is lead, some 90 percent of which comes from leaded gasoline. This toxic metal impairs the kidneys, liver, and reproductive system, and at high levels causes irreversible brain damage. Recent studies suggest that some 64 percent of children in New Delhi and 65–100 percent of children in Shanghai have blood levels of lead above the point at which adverse health effects occur. In Cairo in early 1999, worsening traffic in the city's industrial areas contributed to atmospheric lead levels that exceeded health guidelines by a factor of 11.[82]

Neighborhood layout and transportation affect not just local livability but the resource demands that a city makes

TABLE 3

Transportation Indicators in Selected Cities, by Regional Average, 1990[1]

| Region | Commute to Work[2] | | | Transport Deaths |
| | Driving | Public Transport | Walking/ Cycling | |
	(percent)			(per 100,000)
United States	86.4	9.0	4.6	14.6
Australia	80.4	14.5	5.1	12.0[3]
Canada	74.1	19.7	6.2	6.5[4]
Western Europe	42.8	38.8	18.4	8.8
Developing Asia	38.4	35.7	25.8	13.7
Wealthy Asia	20.1	59.6	20.3	6.6

[1] See endnote 81 for list of cities. [2] Numbers do not total 100 due to rounding.
[3] Average does not include Canberra. [4] Toronto only.
Source: See endnote 81.

on many parts of the planet. Changes in the urban form can lower energy demands from transportation by a factor of 10. Cars devour not just energy but land. Each car needs as much road as 4–8 bicycles and as much parking as 20 bikes. All in all, roads and parking pave over at least one third of car-reliant cities. What often goes unnoticed is that a city's water quality and quantity suffer in proportion to the amount of pavement that covers its watershed.[83]

Moreover, when neighborhoods are spread out at low density, they require more water and sewer pipes, power lines, roads, and building materials. Buildings, which consume roughly 40 percent of materials in the global economy, represent one fourth of the demand for wood worldwide. In the United States, many buildings go unused in inner cities, while new buildings are constructed farther out from the city center. It is a tremendously wasteful phenomenon. For instance, between 1970 and 1990, total metropolitan school enrollment in the Minneapolis and St. Paul area fell by 81,000. During this time, 132 schools were closed in the inner city and closer-in suburbs while 50 new schools were built in remote suburbs.[84]

A recent World Bank study suggests that the high costs of automobile dependence can actually erode economic development. In the United States, a 1998 survey of leading real estate investors and analysts came to a similar conclusion: denser cities that boast alternatives to the car are better investment bets than sprawling suburban agglomerations. Car-choked cities waste time and money. As a senior executive at Bell South on the verge of moving his 13,000 employees into the city of Atlanta from the suburbs observed, the productivity lost in missed planes and missed meetings adds up. The United States has built the most roads at the expense of other travel modes—and drivers in 70 metropolitan areas spend an average 40 hours each sitting in stalled traffic per year. As a result, wasted fuel and lost productivity cost $74 billion annually. New roads attract more cars, so regions that have invested heavily in road construction have fared no better at easing congestion than those that have invested less.[85]

A few cities are beginning to rein in rapacious development, boost parkland, and diversify transportation options. Their tactics include both regulations and market mechanisms to clean up vehicle emissions, give priority to bicycling and rail, and invite developers to build on vacant land within the city rather than on outlying green areas.

Some technical fixes for vehicle pollution, already adopted in most industrial nations, are urgently needed elsewhere. The reduced health risks and car maintenance costs that follow from removing lead from gasoline and requiring catalytic converters far outweigh their expense. For instance, the World Bank estimates that in Manila, basic improvements in vehicles and fuels alone would save more than 2,000 lives and at least $200 million a year in avoided health costs. Even more efficient cars and cleaner fuels than these are on the horizon—ultra-efficient vehicles powered by emissions-free hydrogen fuel cells, for instance. While promising, these innovations will still only address pollution, leaving accidents, congestion, and social inequity untouched. The larger issue of linking transportation to land use planning will be essential to reining in automobile use and making cities livable.[86]

One of the best examples of integrated planning comes from Curitiba, Brazil. In the early 1970s, the city designated several main roadways radiating from the city center as structural axes for busways. Through zoning laws, the city encouraged construction of high-density buildings along these transit corridors. Since then, innovations such as extra-large buses for popular routes and inviting, tube-shaped shelters where passengers pay their fares in advance have added to the system's speed and convenience. The bus stations link to a 150-kilometer network of bike paths. Although Curitiba has one car for every three people, two thirds of all trips in the city are made by bus. Car traffic has declined by 30 percent since 1974, even as the population has doubled.[87]

City planners in Curitiba have also made progress in dealing with the key reason for chaotic urban development in developing countries: 30–60 percent of city populations live in squatter settlements. "The unnamed millions who build, organize and plan illegally are the most important organizers, builders and planners of Third World cities," in the words of Jorge Hardoy and David Satterthwaite. Those who cannot afford a house on the formal market seek out the most precarious slopes and river valleys—places to which it is difficult and costly to extend water pipes and electricity lines. However, opportunities for a better life for the occupants of such settlements do exist in some cities in the form of places already close to transportation and services. Here, low-income sites could be developed, at lower cost. In Curitiba, the city set aside such tracts for informal settlements.[88]

Other leading examples of transportation and land use planning come from Western Europe. In the Netherlands, cities follow a national "ABC" policy to steer new development to easily accessible "A" locations, which are the ones best served by public transit and bicycle paths. And by pursuing a national Bicycle Master Plan, Dutch cities have achieved some of the world's highest rates of bicycling: 30 percent of all urban trips there are made by bike, compared with just 1 percent in U.S. cities. In Stockholm, the city council has planned "transit villages" around suburban rail stations, allowing homes to sprout only a short walk from offices and stores. The walkability of these neighborhoods prompted car trips to fall between 1980 and 1990 as transit use rose.[89]

The U.S. city with the most success at stemming sprawl is Portland, Oregon. A 1973 state law requires the metropolitan area to demarcate an urban growth boundary to allow for future growth without encroaching too far into agricultural or forestland. Planners are now trying to reduce the need for cars within the boundary by requiring most new building to be within a short walk of a transit stop. Revised codes allow for mixed-use development of apartments above stores and forbid "snob zoning" that prohibits the denser type of housing—townhouses and apartment buildings—that can support mass transit ridership.[90]

As Portland demonstrates, compact urban neighborhoods connected by public transport need not be forbidding. The city has fortified its ties to nature by removing freeways that once blocked access to the Willamette River and requiring buildings to step down as they approach the city's eastern edge, in order to protect "view corridors" of Mount Hood. And because suburban development is confined, Portlanders do not have to travel far to enjoy the wilderness. Newman and Kenworthy point out that some of the most population-dense European hubs, such as Paris and Vienna, are among the most aesthetically pleasing cities in the world.[91]

As a sprawl backlash sweeps across the United States, political support is beginning to grow for integrated planning. The "New Urbanists," a band of architects and urban planners who have gained prominence in the 1990s, are promoting walkable neighborhoods connected by rail. Efforts are under way in states such as Maryland—whose "Smart Growth" initiative has entered the national lexicon— California, and New Jersey. A report on the November 1998 U.S. elections for the Brookings Institution by independent consultant Phyllis Myers identified 13 state and 226 local ballot initiatives to rein in suburbia, protect green space, and channel new development toward existing communities. Voters in 31 states approved 72 percent of these measures.[92]

Financial levers can support planning decisions. Among these are road, bridge, tunnel, and parking fees, which all reflect the high cost to society of car use. Singapore leads the world in using tolls to curb traffic. For more than 20 years, downtown-bound drivers have paid a fee that rises during rush hour; since 1998, the fee has been automatically deducted from an electronic card. In the United States, state and national policies are beginning to target parking subsidies, which are worth $31.5 billion a year. For instance, a 1992 California law requires employers who offer free parking to also provide a cash alternative that can be used for public transportation or bicycles; this innovation spurred a 17 percent drop in solo driving at several firms. In 1998, a national transportation act changed the tax code to support such "cash-outs." [93]

Decoupling car ownership from car use can also remove incentives to drive. Once a person pays for a car, he may want to use it as much as possible to get his money's worth. New car-sharing networks, popular in Europe since the late 1980s, circumvent that problem by providing easy access to a car, without the costs of owning or the hassles of renting. Each member pays for a card that opens lockers holding keys to cars parked around the city. Members who call the network to reserve a car are directed to the closest one. The European Car Sharing Network now has participants in more than 50 organizations in over 300 cities in Germany, Austria, Switzerland, and the Netherlands. One of the largest groups, Berlin-based Stattauto, estimates that each of their vehicles replaces five private cars; altogether the fleet eliminates 510,000 kilometers of driving each year. Italy is set to join the club in 1999 with national incentives for cities to organize electric car-sharing services. [94]

Some cities have found a novel way to use the most widespread form of local revenue, the property tax, to promote development of vacant lots within urban areas. Most property taxes fail to do this because they merge two taxes that are at odds with each other—a tax on buildings and a tax on land—into one. The more time and money that a property owner invests in developing a lot and making improvements to the building, the greater the value of that building will be. Also, buildings that require space for elevators and stairs are more expensive to build per square foot of usable space, so taxes on buildings fall disproportionately on taller structures. Thus, taxes on buildings tend to raise rents, disperse construction, and discourage urban redevelopment. In contrast, the worth of the land under the building depends only on location, so the land tax is relatively benign.[95]

By cutting building taxes and taxing only the land, local authorities might promote compact development. Alan Thein Durning and Yoram Bauman of Seattle-based Northwest Environment Watch estimate that by shifting property taxes from building to land value, two counties in Washington state would increase taxes by up to 25 percent on strip malls and moderately reduce taxes on pedestrian shopping districts. The shift would cut taxes by about one third on land-efficient apartments and condominiums and by about 5 percent on single-family residences.[96]

In his book on using market mechanisms to benefit the environment, David Roodman points to towns and cities in much of Denmark and in parts of Australia, Colombia, Indonesia, Jamaica, New Zealand, Pennsylvania, South Africa, and South Korea that have shifted at least part of their property taxes off building and onto land in the past century. In Melbourne, Australia, half of the local governments within the metropolitan area cut the tax on buildings and boosted the tax on land between 1919 and 1986. Today, the districts that do not tax buildings have more of them, which reduces the pressure to build on the city's fringe.[97]

A tax shift from buildings to land may work best given complementary policies that offer incentives to protect surrounding forests and farmland from development as well as policies to encourage "infill" development of lots within the city. For instance, some state and local governments in the

United States have created preservation programs to buy valuable farmland, forest, and wetlands at risk of being lost to suburban development. Limits on suburban expansion like those that Portland has adopted are another type of policy. Fiscal reforms such as ending subsidies—the cornerstone of Maryland's "smart growth" plan—to build roads, schools, and water and sewer infrastructure in outlying areas would also help limit horizontal expansion.[98]

To reduce fringe development, a number of older industrial cities are offering incentives to redevelop vacant or abandoned parcels of land within the metropolitan area. Some of the most sought-after new housing in southern England, for instance, is on such infill sites. One concern, however, is that a former occupant may have been an industrial polluter who left the land contaminated. By offering tax credits and funds for environmental cleanup, cities and higher forms of government can entice buyers to choose a central location rather than a "greenfield"—a strategy that benefits the entire region in the long term. Following the U.S. Environmental Protection Agency's announcement of a federal "brownfields" initiative, some 250 pilot redevelopment efforts have been proposed in U.S. cities.[99]

Districts that do not tax buildings have more of them.

Inner city locations generally have a transportation advantage over outlying areas. A new experiment in home financing in the United States aims to use this attraction to draw people toward transportation nodes. The "location-efficient mortgage," for example, pioneered by the Natural Resources Defense Council, and supported also by the Center for Neighborhood Technology and the Surface Transportation Policy Project, is allowing buyers of location-efficient homes in three test markets—Chicago, Los Angeles, and Seattle—to translate savings in transportation into a larger home loan.[100]

Cities can involve the private sector in financing sustainable transportation systems. In the late nineteenth century, private companies would foot the bill for urban rail construction in return for development rights near the stations. Public funds have paid for such construction in recent years. But now a private company in Portland is negotiating construction of a light rail track to the airport in exchange for a lease to airport land, and numerous other projects are under way elsewhere. The private sector can also help operate public transit. In Curitiba, private companies pay for bus operating costs; the city pays for the roads, lighting, bus stops, and staff to monitor the companies. Copenhagen has even extended the public-private partnership idea to bicycles by maintaining a fleet of 2,300 bikes for public use that is financed through advertising on the wheel surfaces and bicycle frames. The system is popular: organizers estimate that a bicycle is used on average once every eight minutes.[101]

Technophiles have promoted electronic information transfer—e-mail, e-commerce, videoconferencing—as a way to reduce the need to move goods and people, and in so doing to avert transportation-related pollution. Certainly, it is true that these technologies are transforming many aspects of business and personal life, and working at home may reduce the need to travel. But while new information technologies may support planning efforts, they will not obviate the need for integrated transportation and land use.[102]

Telecommuters lured away from urban centers will still need food and services. Transportation and land use planning will be critical to prevent "telesprawl"—people living even farther away from others because they rely on machines for communication. Indeed, by connecting more far-flung people, communications technologies may actually induce more travel. As urban scholar Peter Hall notes, no information technology in history has ever been associated with a net reduction in travel or face-to-face contact: between 1880 and 1910, telephones were paralleled by commuter railways and metropolitan subways; between 1920 and 1940, radios by automobiles and airplanes; and between 1950 and 1970, television by highways and commercial jets. And despite the dazzling advances in communication technology, this pattern may still hold true. Douglas Henton, an economist for a Silicon Valley consulting firm, argues that creative work still occurs mainly in face-to-face exchange, where people live and work in close proximity. The Internet firm Adobe moved its thousands of workers to downtown San Jose, California, rather than developing a greenfield at the edge of Silicon Valley because it felt this appealing urban location would better enable it to attract and retain good workers. So, contrary to what one might expect, there is actually a natural link between the information economy and walkable, mixed-use neighborhoods linked by public transport.[103]

Financing the Sustainable City

Like so many artifacts of civilization, money and finance first arose in cities. Researchers believe that cash first flowed in ancient Mesopotamia as early as 2500 B.C. As many more goods became available in urban centers like Babylon and Ur, bartering became unmanageable, and for the first time in history, people needed a standard medium for setting prices. Today, cities remain the engines of economic growth—generating a disproportionate share of national income—but their problems with money are legion. For the sake of the public good, citizens and local officials alike struggle to harness the money they generate, but all too often it becomes yet another squandered urban resource. Among the obstacles keeping money from constructive uses are lack of support from national governments, poor financial management by city officials, and the outflow of money from a city as banks or store-owners invest in places that inspire more confidence.[104]

Lack of local budgetary control limits the ability of citizens and city officials to make urban environmental concerns a priority. National governments have shifted many responsibilities to city governments in recent years without expanding the ability of local authorities to raise money.

Generally, city governments must still rely on the central government to transfer to them a share of the national tax revenue. And in some countries, the amount of the transfer depends upon the size of the local budget deficit, thus encouraging overspending and mismanagement. If and when the transfers come through, local officials—and the citizens who elect them—may have little say in how they are to be spent. World Bank researchers Roy Bahl and Johannes Linn have found the share of locally generated revenue on the decline in most cities of the developing world.[105]

National governments can even more directly block local efforts to create healthier cities. By subsidizing water and energy, a national government can undermine a city council's building codes to improve efficient use of these resources. And national transportation and land use priorities can similarly foil local environmental goals. For instance, in the United States, metropolitan areas such as Portland, Oregon, that have tried to constrain sprawl have historically been thwarted by national transportation policy that offers far more money for road building than for mass transit.[106]

Encouraging reforms in the 1990s include the Intermodal Surface Transportation Efficiency Act (ISTEA) and its successor, the Transportation Equity Act of the 21st Century (TEA-21)—which set aside a small but important sum for alternatives to highways—and Clean Air Act revisions that withhold highway money from cities that do not meet air quality standards. In much the same way as these policies promote better transportation and land use in the United States, national energy policies in Japan and Europe are triggering the boom in urban rooftop solar systems.[107]

Cities usually have at least two types of tools to raise their own revenue—fees and taxes—although their ability to levy them varies widely. In most industrial countries and a few developing countries, cities are also able to use a third device: municipal bonds. In a sampling of world cities weighted more toward those in the developing world, local taxes were found to be the most important source of revenue.

(See Figure 3.) Partnerships with the private sector and communities can also help local authorities achieve their goals.
The challenge is to figure out which tools local governments
are best equipped to use, and how they can best exploit them
to benefit both the environment and their budget.[108]

One of the best ways for cities to close the gap between
revenue and expenditure would be to charge adequate fees
for the local services they provide. It stands to reason that if
cities are required to supply services, they should also be
allowed to charge for them. Water provision, waste collection, and transportation have a profound impact on natural
resources and quality of life—yet they are usually underpriced. Various fees are effective in meeting both economic
and environmental goals. Fees for unsorted household
garbage, for example, have bolstered urban recycling efforts
in a number of industrial nations. The success of water conservation programs from Bogor, Indonesia, to Boston,
Massachusetts, has hinged on charging higher prices. Rather

FIGURE 3

Sources of Local Revenue, Average of Selected Cities Worldwide, 1993

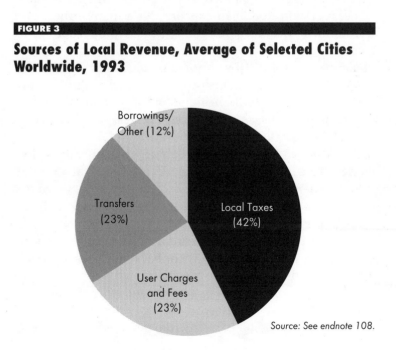

Source: See endnote 108.

than maintain artificially low prices for all, water authorities or electric utilities can provide targeted subsidies, such as loans or grants to help the poorest families pay for the initial hook-up, which is often the most prohibitive cost. Another tactic is to raise fees on parking to discourage driving and help fund public transportation. Local authorities can also be far more discriminating in their use of sewer and road subsidies. By taking away support for extension of sewer lines and roads—or by charging fees to install them—local governments can make developers pay the full costs of building on greenfield sites.[109]

As for taxes, central governments generally want to limit competition from local governments for broad-based taxes on personal income and payroll. That cities are denied this taxing power is not necessarily bad news for local officials, because these taxes in effect discourage work and investment and do nothing to improve the environment. The one tax that may yield great benefits for cities—and that cities are uniquely qualified to control—is the tax on land value. As David Roodman explains, "If a map of the world were drawn with each hectare scaled in proportion to its commercial value, cities would nearly fill the continents. The lion's share of land value, and hence the revenue potential from taxing it, lies in towns and cities." Shifting property taxes off of buildings and onto land may promote development of vacant lots in central areas, as discussed in the previous section.[110]

Municipal bonds, which allow governments to borrow money from the public to finance projects that promote public welfare, may offer local governments an opportunity to obtain more cash up front than they could normally get through fees or taxes. When private investors buy the bonds, they give the city immediate cash for a given project, and the government promises to pay them back at a later date with interest. Bonds were created by governments in response to the challenges posed by rapid urbanization in Britain and Europe in the late nineteenth century. Governments first issued bonds to build infrastructure such as water systems and bridges, but in the United States these devices are increasingly being used by state and local governments to fund the creation of parks and the purchase of valuable farmland and open space. For instance, Florida has raised $3 billion to buy land and safeguard it from development.[111]

Cities can only use bonds as a third option if they are already using the other two. A city can issue two types of bonds that differ in the way that the municipality pays back its debt to investors. Cities repay revenue bondholders by assessing user fees collected from the specific project—for instance, a water or power supply system. But they repay the owners of general obligation bonds for projects such as sewers, where cost recovery is not easily tied to use, by levying taxes. So for bonds to work, a city must have the authority to raise fees and taxes. In addition, governments need access to a financial market where bonds can be exchanged. Thus, municipal bonds are an important revenue source for cities in industrial countries, but are not available to most local authorities in developing countries.[112]

With insufficient public revenue to meet the rising demand for services, cash-strapped local authorities have increasingly relied on the resourcefulness of local communities and NGOs as well as the profit-making drive of the private sector. Examples of successful public-private partnership range from community-based recycling in Bandung, Indonesia, to private-sector-financed light rail in Portland, Oregon. Such projects have successfully managed to match the need for urban services with the demand for jobs—which mayors worldwide cite as their most pressing concern, according to a recent UNDP survey. UNDP's recently established Public-Private Partnerships for the Urban Environment program aims to help cities in developing countries turn environmental problems into viable business opportunities in water, waste, and energy services.[113]

As such programs recognize, however, grassroots activists and private businesses cannot substitute for a responsible government. Alliances between local government and private enterprises must be actual partnerships, in which local authorities acknowledge their responsibility for safeguarding public welfare. When the resources of the private sector far outweigh those of the city, local authorities may be unable to oversee the companies' activities and to ensure the provision of service to all. These concerns are not new: in the industrial cities of the nineteenth century, people complained that rail companies neglected projects that would benefit the public. Today, governments still run into trouble as they try to harness the private sector to meet public needs. For instance, governments in booming East Asian nations turned to foreign capital markets to finance urban infrastructure in the 1980s and 1990s, but their plans for projects faltered as private investors fled during the financial crisis. And in the United States, mayors who commit limited government revenues to repay debt for sports stadiums hamper their ability to pay for schools, transportation systems, and other crucial public investments. In one such effort, an unsuccessful bid to keep its football team, the U.S. city of Cleveland offered $175 million to renovate its stadium, yet closed 11 schools the same year for lack of funding.[114]

Schemes to generate large bundles of cash appeal to local leaders, but a better long-term strategy would be to focus on collecting taxes and fees before resorting to borrowing money. This was demonstrated in Ahmedabad, India, a city with long-standing air and water pollution from a textile industry that suffered a major economic crisis in the 1980s with the closure of several mills. A talented municipal commissioner began a campaign in the early 1990s to balance the city's budget by eliminating costly corruption, raising utility rates, and collecting taxes. As a result, by 1996, the city boasted a substantial surplus, and it used the new funds to initiate a host of projects to improve the local environment and public health. As environmental health rebounded, so too did the climate for investment, which may ultimately attract outside money to solving Ahmedabad's problems. With advice from the U.S. Agency for International Development, the city has floated India's first municipal bond, which will finance improvements in water and sewer infrastructure.[115]

A key problem that poor neighborhoods in cities face is the outflow of money. Just as taxes and fees must come before bonds, support for local business is a precondition for attracting outside investors to a city. Locally owned businesses are important because they are more likely to spend the money they take in within the neighborhood or city—and this "recycling" of funds nurtures the local economy. The goal of some "community enterprise zone" programs in the United States has been to lure outside businesses with low taxes, but a historical review found that the most significant job creation occurred when such programs focused on helping local businesses expand rather than on attracting outside businesses to impoverished areas. The same local restaurants and stores that residents would support make a neighborhood attractive to larger enterprises. Harvard economist Michael Porter points out that even the poorest neighborhoods have competitive advantages, whether it is local demand for a particular service, strategic proximity to downtown offices, a budding regional cluster of businesses nearby in a particular industry, or the availability of local workers. Local entrepreneurs might be able to take advantage of such opportunities, but they lack something that larger companies already have: access to financing.[116]

Small-scale lending programs by nonprofit groups and community reinvestment by traditional banks can help recycle local money and promote "green" businesses from recycling to urban farming. Small loans give a chance to poor entrepreneurs who lack the collateral a traditional bank would require. A microcredit model, pioneered by Mohammed Yunus' Grameen Bank in rural Bangladesh, has succeeded by lending to circles of friends. If one of them neglects to pay back the loan, the others are penalized, so peer pressure works in the bank's favor. Adapting microcredit to urban areas may take some work, however. Because the system relies on people's reputations as collateral, it might be more difficult to establish among transient urban poor. Nevertheless, a handful of urban nonprofit groups have applied Grameen's "lending-circle" approach in the United States. For instance, Chicago's Women's Self-Employment Project (WSEP) only lends to groups of single women from the same neighborhood who agree to help each other with their business plans. Also in Chicago, the South Shore Bank has pioneered another way to keep money within a community. Most banks accept savings from people in slums, but lend money elsewhere—and by predicting a neighborhood's demise, they help ensure it. Since 1983, South Shore has profitably extended loans to refurbish homes in poor neighborhoods.[117]

Building Political Strength

Citizens, the ancient Athenians realized, are the best people to identify priorities for action in their own cities. If cities are to become more sustainable, people must take action in the neighborhoods where they live. Most of the urban environmental success stories came about when citizens identified various problems and the links between them in order to pin down cause and effect. A charismatic mayor in Curitiba, for instance, saw that chaotic development and poor public transportation conspired to worsen air pollution: car use increased as buildings sprouted far from bus stops. By winning popular backing for a new bus system, he demonstrated that when citizens understand such connections, they often support or even demand change. This was also the case in Chattanooga, where citizens came together in the 1980s to identify problems and choose plans to solve them in a city-wide "visioning" process that led to the city's dramatic environmental turnaround. And in Copenhagen, an environmentally literate populace has long pushed for green initiatives, from water recycling, to composting, to bicycle lanes.

Most urban residents support strong environmental policies, but wealthy interest groups and corrupt officials often skew local political decisions. National legislatures in resource-rich countries such as the United States, Canada, and Brazil tend to be disproportionately influenced by extractive industries that operate in rural areas. City councils, in contrast, must answer to requests for environmental services. The multi-billion-dollar market for water and sewage, waste management, air quality control, and other environmental services is largely urban, according to the Organisation for Economic Co-operation and Development (OECD). However, legal campaign contributions or illegal bribes by developers can sway city officials.[118]

Nonetheless, compared to higher forms of government, local government is smaller and closer to the people, so organized citizens have a better chance of changing the status quo. For instance, in the 1990s, two citizens groups in Portland, Oregon, blocked a proposed highway by publicizing the fact that computer models of traffic prediction did not take into account the benefits of walkable and bikeable neighborhoods. Updating the software, these advocates showed that over 20 years, development geared toward transit, pedestrians, and cyclists would result in 18 percent less highway congestion than building a new bypass would.[119]

More recently, organized citizens in a handful of local elections in the United States in November 1998 took a different tack to sever the tie between local officials and the housing and construction industries that help propel urban sprawl. In Southern California, Ventura County citizens took power away from county supervisors by adopting a strict measure to create urban growth boundaries. Now, if Ventura County officials want to rezone agricultural and rural land outside the boundaries for development before the year 2020, they will have to receive voter approval. Similarly, in Scottsdale, Arizona, voter consent will be required before authorities can sell or lease land in the Sonoran Preserve. In March 1999, a congressman from Portland, Oregon, remarked that he had seen "more political progress toward building livable U.S. cities in the last 30 weeks than in the last 30 years."[120]

When citizens have insufficient understanding of the causes of local problems, the political process suffers. Many cities lack the basic demographic and environmental data needed to unveil the links between urban trends and environmental problems. In 1993, a Ford Foundation review of urban research in the developing world found that the "urban environment" was listed as a priority area for study in nearly every report they unearthed, but that only 2–3 percent of the research actually had an environmental focus.[121]

Fortunately, support for the needed data collection is gathering momentum. For instance, in the 1990s, the Urban Management Programme—a joint effort of UNDP, the U.N. Centre on Human Settlements (UNCHS, or Habitat), and the World Bank—formulated a "rapid urban environmental assessment" survey to identify key environmental indicators in cities of the developing world. And in June 1996, representatives from 171 nations and 579 cities met in Istanbul for the second U.N. Conference on Human Settlements, Habitat II, where they called for cities that are "safer, healthier and more livable, equitable, sustainable and productive." Delegates signed on to a Habitat Agenda that echoed the call made at the 1992 Earth Summit in Rio for cities to adopt local versions of the "Agenda 21" for global environment and development that nations endorsed in Rio. These "Local Agenda 21's" are campaigns to identify environmental problems and plans to remedy them. So far, cities with Local Agenda 21's are generally those that have strong support from the national level. A 1997 survey showed that 82 percent of known Local Agenda 21 initiatives were concentrated in 11 countries with national campaigns sponsored by government or country-wide municipal associations.[122]

The Habitat Agenda charges Habitat with compiling data to review progress since the summit. The database now includes indicators on population, income, water, waste, housing, and transportation for 237 cities in 110 countries. To expand the effort, Habitat has been assembling government experts, university scholars, and independent researchers in a Global Urban Observatory Network.[123]

Armed with basic data, cities and communities can formulate more specific indicators to measure their progress toward becoming more livable and sustainable. The choice of what to measure will depend on the city. There is a great deal of theoretical literature on the subject. For instance, Tufts University researcher Elizabeth Kline has suggested four categories of indicators—economic security, ecological integrity, quality of life, and empowerment—to help communities decide what indicators to devise. And the Balaton Group, an international network of scholars devoted to sustainable development, has put forth another framework to reflect a community's natural capital, built capital, human and social capital, and well-being.[124]

In the hands of the public, information can be a potent political tool. For example, Beijing officials released data on air pollution for the first time in February 1998. By June 1998, according to the *New York Times*, "people who six months ago might have peered out the window and seen fog, or *wu*, now realize that it is pollution, or *wuran*," and they support local government efforts to clean up the air. Surveys of the users **ICLEI disseminates information about the 2,000-plus cities now working on Local Agenda 21's.** of city services such as water and transportation can reveal key problems with city government itself. In India, an enterprising NGO, the Public Affairs Centre, surveyed residents of major cities about the quality of municipal services and published its findings in city "report cards" that were released to the media. Among the problems documented was widespread corruption in Bangalore, with one in eight citizens reporting that they had to pay bribes to receive attention.[125]

A tool that is well suited to expose the links between urban population and environmental problems is a geographic information system (GIS), which portrays data in a map form. A GIS undergirds the U.S. experiment in location-efficient mortgages, quantifying savings at specific addresses. Another GIS database, in Quito, Ecuador, integrates epidemiological data from the Department of Health with data on water and waste service provision and data on poverty and employment, thus providing a useful picture of the environmental and social sources of ill health.[126]

When maps show people environmental problems in their backyard, they can spur citizen action. By integrating geographic information on polluting factories, major roadways, and air and water quality monitoring, the pollution control agency in Rio de Janeiro State created detailed maps that show the sources of pollution. These maps are available to the public, who can then become actively involved in pollution control by protesting to industries directly.[127]

In the United States, maps are being used in the effort to unite urban regions and combat sprawl. Minnesota state legislator Myron Orfield created maps that show the decline of central Minneapolis and St. Paul and their inner suburbs, the rise of affluent outer suburbs, and the subsidies in public infrastructure that have flowed from the central city to the outlying areas. And in Maryland, a study undertaken in the 1990s combined satellite images, historical maps and census data in a GIS to create maps of urban cover that give snapshots of certain years in the centuries between 1792 and 1992, and a video animation showing Baltimore and Washington merging into one massive agglomeration by the 1990s. The governor of Maryland credited the video with helping him win legislative approval for his anti-sprawl initiatives.[128]

Another source of useful information is the experience of other cities. Nineteenth-century sanitary reforms gained momentum as scientists and local authorities from different cities compared notes. Such exchange is just as essential today. Various types of collaboration between cities to promote sustainable development have been rapidly multiplying in the 1990s. (See Appendix.) In 1990, the Toronto-based International Council on Local Environmental Initiatives (ICLEI) was formed to serve as the environmental arm of the world's oldest association of municipalities, the International Union of Local Authorities. As a clearinghouse, ICLEI disseminates information about the 2,000-plus cities in 64 countries that are now working on Local Agenda 21's. In a similar vein, one of the most immediate outcomes of the Istanbul Habitat meeting was a database of "Best Practices," which now contains more than 650 urban success stories. Since each city is unique, an innovation from one might be adapted, rather than precisely replicated, in another.[129]

Direct contact between local authorities from different cities speeds information exchange. For instance, municipal water experts from Nancy, France, who traveled to Costa Rica in 1991, helped design the watershed protection plan in San José that was discussed earlier. In recent years, networks for sustainable cities have proliferated, organized by existing municipal associations, NGOs, national governments, and international agencies. The New York-based Mega-Cities Project, one of the most prominent such NGOs, was founded in 1987 to promote exchange between officials from the world's largest cities. It has brought ideas about buses from Curitiba to New York and innovations in community-based recycling from Cairo to Bombay and Manila.[130]

In some cases, governments or international agencies fund sustainable city networks. For instance, the World Bank and the European Investment Bank brought mayors of cities bordering the Mediterranean together in Barcelona in 1991 to launch the Mediterranean Coastal Cities Network. The lending institutions, along with UNDP, help the cities gather data on environmental problems and devise solutions, as well as exchange information.[131]

Europe has some of the strongest city exchange programs. More than 100 European city leaders convened in Aalborg, Denmark, in 1994 to inaugurate the European Sustainable Cities and Towns Campaign, which is supported by several municipal associations in Europe and by ICLEI and the World Health Organization as well. Mayors pledged to work together to reduce the car travel, inefficient industrial production, and wasteful consumption that make their cities "essentially responsible for many environmental problems humankind is facing." Some 800 cities, 600 of them in Europe, have joined WHO's Healthy Cities Campaign, which helps municipalities devise long-term strategies for becoming greener and healthier. Another group, Energie-Cités, is a European network of more than 150 cities that share information on urban energy planning.[132]

A broader-based initiative on energy, led by ICLEI, was initially spearheaded by the City of Toronto and supported by 13 other cities in Canada, the United States, Europe, and Turkey. Their initial research effort blossomed into a full-fledged campaign in 1993 to help local governments conceive and implement action plans to reduce their greenhouse emissions. City-to-city exchanges are not as politically charged as negotiations among nations, so cities have been able to make stronger commitments to reduce their emissions than their national governments have done under the climate treaty. As of April 1999, some 300 cities, responsible for at least 7 percent of global emissions, had pledged to lower their emissions to 20 percent below a baseline target by 2005–2010—a goal that far exceeds the 5 percent cut by industrial nations agreed to by national governments in Kyoto, Japan, in 1997. The campaign initially targeted cities in the industrial world, but is now recruiting worldwide and boasts a diverse group of developing-country members, including Hanoi, Belo Horizonte (Brazil), Tehran, Calcutta, and Suva City (Fiji). City governments that have signed on to the campaign have made real progress. Copenhagen, Saarbrucken, and Toronto had reduced their emissions 7–22 percent below 1990 levels by 1996.[133]

A major way that local politics affects the environment relates to the structure of local government itself. Rarely does one government entity correspond to an entire metropolitan region. Often, districts within a metropolis compete with each other for development that will boost tax revenue, and in so doing they push built-up areas out over forests and farmland, pave over watersheds, and invite air pollution from increased car use. The problem is particularly acute in U.S. cities. Up until the 1920s, they would commonly expand by annexation, but now politically powerful suburbs block them. The Washington, DC, metropolitan area is one of the most fragmented, encompassing several counties in two states and one federal district—and it is also one of the most sprawling. On the other hand, Portland, Oregon, which has made notable environmental progress, is also the only place in the United States where a city and its suburbs elect a common government that has the power to look out for the interests of the entire metropolitan region.[134]

Proponents of "metropolitanism" are gaining new allies as the economic rationale for united urban regions becomes clearer. David Rusk, former mayor of Albuquerque, New Mexico, has shown that regions with less political division between cities and suburbs are also less segregated along lines of race and class and are economically healthier than politically fragmented regions. Rusk compared the U.S. cities that most expanded their limits between 1960 and 1990 to include a portion of their suburbs to those cities whose boundaries remained fairly constant. In the cities that were most cut off from their suburbs, average income had fallen to 66 percent of suburban levels by 1990, and the average bond rating was "A." In contrast, cities that incorporated more of their suburbs had an average income that was 91 percent of suburban levels and a higher—"AA"—bond rating. Thus, inner city boosters and residents of decaying older suburbs seeking to direct investment toward existing infrastructure are allying with environmentalists who are attempting to protect fringe areas from development.[135]

Metropolitan cooperation is also budding in Curitiba, Brazil. Despite its planning success, Curitiba has suffered from a lack of cooperation with the 13 municipalities that surround it. Urban analysts Jonas Rabinovitch and Josef Leitmann note that ongoing problems—with sanitation and transportation, for instance—generally stem from the fact that cities cannot be managed in isolation from neighboring municipalities. However, there are signs that the greater Curitiba metropolitan region is becoming more united since Jaime Lerner, the former Curitiba mayor, was elected mayor of the state of Paraná five years ago. Under his direction, a regional bus system is up and running for the first time.[136]

In the late nineteenth and early twentieth centuries, people who reflected on life-threatening urban pollution—Dickens, Howard, and Le Corbusier among them—feared that cities might eventually self-destruct. Today, cities account for a far greater share of the world's population than they did in the early 1900s, and their resource use is threatening to undermine the planet's life support systems. Thus, the threat is now global as well as local. But efforts to overcome the financial and political barriers to sustainable city planning have one thing in common: the dynamism of committed people trading ideas and working together. This concentration of human energy allowed cities to give birth to human civilization—and may ultimately save it.

Appendix

Some Organizations that Support Sustainable Cities

United Nations Programs

U.N. Centre for Human Settlements (Habitat)
As the U.N. agency responsible for human settlements, Nairobi-based Habitat is involved in the following initiatives to promote sustainable cities:

Best Practices Database
website: http://www.bestpractices.org
This compendium of case studies of sustainable city building from around the world is updated annually.

Sustainable Cities Programme
P.O. Box 30030
Nairobi, Kenya
tel: 254 2 62 3225
fax: 254 2 62 3715
e-mail: scp@unchs.org
website: http://unep/unon/unchs/scp
This joint undertaking of Habitat and the U.N. Environment Programme promotes a sustainable urban environment in developing countries.

Global Urban Observatory
tel: 254 2 62 3184
fax: 254 2 62 4263
e-mail: guo@unchs.org
website: http://www.urban observatory.org
This new worldwide network of researchers, organized by Habitat, is compiling urban indicators and best practices. Its website contains a database of urban indicators and *State of the World's Cities: 1999*, HS/C/17/2/Add.1 (Nairobi: Habitat, 1999).

Public Private Partnerships for the Urban Environment Programme
UNDP/PPP Headquarters
304 E. 45th St., 10th Floor
New York, NY 10017 USA
tel: (212) 906 5767
fax: (212) 906 6973
e-mail: pppue@undp.org

website: http://sdnhq.undp.org/ppp
Organized by UNDP, this program helps cities in the developing world find private sector partners to provide critical environmental services.

World Health Organisation Center for Urban Health/Healthy Cities Project
8 Scherfigsvej
2100 Copenhagen, Denmark
tel: 45 39 17 17 17
fax: 45 39 17 18 60
website: http://www.who.dk/healthy-cities
This project aims to put urban health on the agenda of policymakers.

City Networks

The International Council for Local Environmental Initiatives (ICLEI)
City Hall East Tower 8th Floor
Toronto, Ontario M5H 2N2 Canada
tel: (416) 392-1462
fax: (416) 392-1478
e-mail: iclei@iclei.org
website: http://www.iclei.org
An association of local governments, ICLEI serves as a clearing-house for information and spearheads Local Agenda 21 and climate change campaigns. The European Good Practice Information Service, the European arm of ICLEI's clearinghouse, is at http://cities21.com/europractice.

Mega-Cities Project
915 Broadway, Suite 1601
New York, NY 10010 USA
tel: (212) 979 7350
fax: (212) 979 7624
e-mail: megacity@igc.apc.org
website: http://www.megacities.org
This non-profit group brings together civil society, business, government, media, and academic leaders from the world's largest cities to spur transfer of urban innovations.

International City/County Management Association (ICMA)
777 North Capitol St., NE, Suite 500
Washington, DC 20002-4201 USA

tel: (202) 289 4262
fax: (202) 962 3500
website: http://icma.org
This organization represents managers in local governments around the world and publishes the *Cities International* newsletter quarterly in English, Spanish, and Russian.

Car-Free Cities
18 Square de Meeus
B-1050-Bruxelles, Belgium
tel: 32 2 552 0874
fax: 32 2 552 08 89
This project to reduce urban car reliance is organized by the European Union-sponsored Eurocities network.

CityNet
International Organization Centre 5F
Pacifico-Yokohama
Minato Mirai, Nishi-ku
Yokohama 220-0012 Japan
tel: 81 45 223 2161
fax: 81 45 223 2162
e-mail: citynet@po.iijnet.or.jp
website: http://www2.itjit.ne.jp/~citynet
Local governments, NGOs, national government organizations, and research and training institutes join CityNet to promote local urban improvement initiatives in the Asia-Pacific region. *City Voice*, the group's newsletter, appears 3–4 times a year.

The Urban Agriculture Network (TUAN)
1711 Lamont St., NW
Washington, DC 20010 USA
tel: (202) 483 8130
fax: (202) 986 6732
e-mail: urbanag@compuserve.com
Jac Smit, TUAN's president, is a co-author of the first study of urban agriculture worldwide, *Urban Agriculture: Food, Jobs, and Sustainable Cities* (New York: UNDP, 1996).

Smart Growth Network
website: http://www.smartgrowth.org
This U.S. coalition of developers, planners, government officials, lending institutions, community development organizations, archi-

tects, environmentalists and community activists is sponsored by the Environmental Protection Agency's Urban and Economic Development Division.

Research Institutes

Instituto de Pesquisa e Planejamento Urbano de Curitiba (IPPUC)
Rua Bom Jesus 669 Juveve
80035-010 Curitiba PR Brazil
tel: 55 41 252 6780
fax: 55 41 252 6679
e-mail: ippucdoc@curitiba.arauc.br
This institute researches sustainable urban development in Curitiba, Brazil.

Danish Town Planning Institute
Peder Skrams Gade 2 B
DK-1054 Copenhagen K Denmark
tel: 45 33 13 72 81
fax: 45 33 14 34 35
e-mail: dantown@inet.uni-c.dk
website: http://www.byplanlab.dk
This private foundation serves as the hub of an urban ecology network and distributes the book *Urban Ecology—Greater Copenhagen* (Copenhagen: Danish Town Planning Institute, 1996).

The European Academy of the Urban Environment
Bismarckallee 46-48
D-14193 Berlin, Germany
tel: 49 30 89 59 99 0
fax: 49 30 89 59 99 19
e-mail: husch@eaue.de
website: http://www.eaue.de
A nonprofit institute set up by the Berlin Senat, EAUE stimulates cooperation on sustainable development among European cities and maintains an Internet database of "best practice" case studies.

Urban Ecology
405 14th St., Suite 900
Oakland, CA 94612 USA
tel: (510) 251 6330
fax: (510) 251 2117
e-mail: ueexecdir@igc.apc.org

website: http://www.urbanecology.org
This membership organization publishes a quarterly journal, *Urban Ecologist*, on cities around the world, and a semi-monthly newsletter, *Sustainable Activist*, on the San Francisco Bay Area.

Institute for Local Self-Reliance
2425 18th St., NW
Washington, DC 20009-2096 USA
tel: (202) 232 4108
fax: (202) 332 0463
website: http://www.ilsr.org
This organization does research and works with citizen groups, governments, and private businesses to extract the maximum value from local resources.

Institute for Policy Studies
733 15th St., NW, Suite 1020
Washington, DC 20005 USA
tel: (202) 234 9382
fax: (202) 387 7915
website: http://www.igc.apc.org/ifps
Michael Shuman, who leads the Institute's Sustainable Communities Program, has written *Going Local* (New York: Free Press, 1998) about community self-reliance.

The Lincoln Institute of Land Policy
113 Brattle St.
Cambridge, MA 02138-3400 USA
tel: (617) 661 3016 or (800) 526 3873
fax: (617) 661 7235 or (800) 526-3944
website: http://www.lincolninst.edu
This nonprofit and tax-exempt school focuses on land policy, including land economics and land taxation.

The Brookings Center on Urban and Metropolitan Policy
1775 Massachusetts Ave., NW
Washington, DC 20036 USA
tel: (202) 797 6000
fax: (202) 797 2965
website: http://www.brookings.edu/es/urban/urban.htm
This center produces policy analysis to inform state and federal policymakers in the United States.

The Comparative Urban Studies Project (CUSP)
Woodrow Wilson International Center for Scholars
1300 Pennsylvania Ave., NW SI MRC 0515
Washington, DC 20523 USA
tel: (202) 691 4235
fax: (202) 691 4247
e-mail: rosanchr@wwic.si.edu
website: http://wwics.si.edu/THEMES/URBAN/
CUSPWEB1.HTM
This project connects urban research worldwide to policymaking through conferences and publications.

Community Economic Development Centre
Simon Fraser University
Burnaby, BC, Canada, V5A 1S6
tel: (604) 291-5850
fax: (604) 291-5473
e-mail: cedc@sfu.ca
website: http://www.sfu.ca/cedc
Mark Roseland, the director of this program, has written a guidebook for citizens and local officials, *Toward Sustainable Communities: Resources for Citizens and Their Governments* (Gabriola, Island, BC, Canada: New Society Publishers, 1998).

Other Organizations in North America

Surface Transportation Policy Project (STTP)
1100 17th St., NW, 10th Floor
Washington, DC 20036 USA
tel: (202) 466 2636
fax: (202) 466 2247
e-mail: stpp@transact.org
websites: http:www.transact.org and http://www.tea21.org
A coalition of local government officials, planners, community development organizations, and advocacy groups, STTP works to improve U.S. transportation policy.

Natural Resources Defense Coucil (NRDC)
40 West 20th St.
New York, NY 10011 USA
tel: (212) 727 2700
website: http://www.nrdc.org
The urban program of this national organization has local projects

in Los Angeles and New York, where it is working with the Banana Kelly neighborhood association in the South Bronx to build an urban paper recycling mill.

Sierra Club
85 Second St., 2nd Floor
San Francisco, CA 94105-3441 USA
tel: (415) 977 5500
fax: (415) 977 5799
website: <http://www.sierraclub.org/transportation/index. htm
This group launched a nationwide "Challenge to Sprawl Campaign" in 1998.

Environmental Defense Fund (EDF)
1875 Connecticut Ave., NW
Washington, DC 20009 USA
tel: (202) 387 3500
fax: (202) 234 6049
website: http://www.edf.org
EDF promotes sustainable cities through its programs in energy, global and regional air, and transportation.

Trust for Public Lands (TPL)
116 New Montgomery St., 4th Floor
San Francisco, CA 94105 USA
tel: (415) 495 4014
fax: (415) 495 4103
website: http://www.tpl.org
TPL preserves open space, parks, and gardens in and around cities.

1000 Friends of Oregon
534 SW Third Ave., Suite 300
Portland, OR 97204 USA
tel: (503) 497-1000
fax: (503) 223-0073
website: http://www.teleport.com/~friends
This citizens' group has promoted sustainable urban development in Portland and other Oregon cities since 1975.

Sprawl Watch Clearinghouse
1100 17th St., NW, 10th Floor
Washington, DC 20036 USA
tel: (202) 974 5133

fax: (202) 466 2247
e-mail: allison@sprawlwatch.org
website: http://www.sprawlwatch.org
This newly formed resource center helps grassroots organizations,
public officials, developers, planners, policymakers, and architects
revitalize existing communities and limit urban sprawl.

Center for Neighborhood Technology
2125 W. North Ave.
Chicago, IL 60647 USA
tel: (312) 278 4800
e-mail: info@cnt.org
website: http://www.cnt.org
This group aims to link economic and community development
with ecological improvement and publishes *The Neighborhood
Works,* a bimonthly magazine.

Partners for Livable Communities
1429 21st St., NW
Washington, DC 20036 USA
tel: (202) 887 5990
fax: (202) 466 4845
e-mail: partners@livable.com
website: http://www.livable.com
This nonprofit organization works to promote livable communities
through technical assistance, leadership training, workshops,
research, and publications.

City Farmer
318 Homer St., Suite 801
Vancouver, BC, Canada VSB 2VC
tel: (604) 685-5832
e-mail: cityfarm@unix.ubc.ca
website: http://www.cityfarmer.org

Notes

1. Christopher Elvidge et al., "Mapping City Lights with Night-time Data from the DMSP Operational Linescan System," *Photogrammetric Engineering and Remote Sensing*, June 1997; Christopher Elvidge et al., "Satellite Inventory of Human Settlements Using Nocturnal Radiation Emissions: A Contribution for the Global Tool Chest," *Global Change Biology*, vol. 3 (1997). Map from National Geophysical Data Center, National Oceanic and Atmospheric Administration, Boulder, Colorado. See also "Nighttime Lights of the World dataset," <http://www.ngdc.noaa.gov/dmsp>, viewed 14 April 1999.

2. Urban population in 1900 from Clive Ponting, *A Green History of the World* (New York: Penguin Books, 1991); urban population in 2006 from United Nations (U.N.), *World Urbanization Prospects: the 1996 Revision* (New York: 1998); United States and Indonesia from U.N., *World Population Prospects: the 1998 Revision*, Volume I, Comprehensive Tables, draft (New York: 1998).

3. Charles Dickens, *Hard Times* (New York: Bantam Books, reissue, 1981); Peter Keating, "The Metropolis in Literature," in Anthony Sutcliffe, ed., *Metropolis 1890–1940* (Chicago: University of Chicago Press, 1984); Tertius Chandler, *Four Thousand Years of Urban Growth: An Historical Census* (Lewiston, NY: Edwin Mellen Press, 1987).

4. World Resources Institute (WRI), U.N. Environment Programme (UNEP), U.N. Development Programme (UNDP), and World Bank, *World Resources 1996–97* (New York: Oxford University Press, 1996). Figure for India in 1995 from Priti Kumar et al., "Death in the Air," *Down to Earth*, 15 November 1997. Kumar's estimate is based on the model used in Carter Brandon and Kirsten Hommann, "The Cost of Inaction: Valuing the Economy-Wide Cost of Environmental Degradation in India," presented at the Modeling Global Sustainability conference, United Nations University, Tokyo, October 1995. Brandon and Hommann used air pollution data in 36 cities in either 1991 or 1992 to obtain an estimate of annual air pollution-related deaths. China from "China Adopts Effective Measures to Curb Pollution," *Xinhua News Agency*, 14 October 1996; "Authorities Reveal 3 Million Deaths Linked to Illness from Urban Air Pollution," *International Environment Reporter*, 30 October 1996; children from Devra Davis et al., "Children at Risk from Current Patterns of Global Air Pollution" (draft), presented at the Annual Meeting of the American Association for the Advancement of Science, Anaheim, CA, 24 January 1999; WRI, "Study Reports Children Globally Facing Major Health Risks from Air Pollution," press release (Washington, DC: 24 January 1999).

5. Mathis Wackernagel and William Rees, *Our Ecological Footprint: Reducing Human Impact on the Earth* (Philadelphia, PA: New Society Publishers, 1996); Herbert Girardet, "Cities and the Biosphere," paper presented at UNDP

Roundtable, The Next Millennium: Cities for People in a Globalizing World, Marmaris, Turkey, 19–21 April 1996; International Institute for Environment and Development (IIED), *Citizen Action to Lighten Britain's Ecological Footprints*, report prepared for the U.K. Department of Environment (London: IIED, 1995).

6.   Calculations based on urban population from U.N., *World Urbanization Prospects: the 1996 Revision*, op. cit. note 2; share of GDP from industry and services from World Bank, *World Development Indicators 1997*, on CD-ROM (Washington, DC: 1997) and World Bank, *World Bank Indicators 1998* (Washington, DC: 1998); carbon emissions from G. Marland et al., "Global, Regional, and National CO_2 Emission Estimates from Fossil Fuel Burning, Cement Production, and Gas Flaring: 1751–1995 (revised March 1999)," Oak Ridge National Laboratory, <http://cdiac.esd.ornl.gov>, viewed 22 April 1999; industrial roundwood consumption from U.N. Food and Agriculture Organization (FAO), *FAOSTAT Statistics Database*, <http://apps.fao.org>; water from I.A. Shiklomanov, "Global Water Resources," *Nature and Resources*, vol. 26, no. 3 (1990); climate change implications from J.T. Houghton et al., eds., *Climate Change 1995: The Science of Climate Change*, Contribution of Working Group I to the Second Assessment Report of the Intergovernmental Panel on Climate Change (Cambridge, U.K.: Cambridge University Press, 1996); deforestation and loss of biological diversity implications from Emil Salim and Ola Ullsten, *Our Forests, Our Future*, Report of the World Commission on Forests and Sustainable Development (Cambridge, U.K: Cambridge University Press, 1999); water implications from Sandra Postel, *Pillar of Sand* (New York: W.W. Norton & Company, 1999) and Peter Gleick, *The World's Water 1998–1999: The Biennial Report on Freshwater Resources* (Washington, DC: Island Press, 1998).

7.   Abel Wolman, "The Metabolism of Cities," *Scientific American*, September 1965; Herbert Girardet, *Cities: New Directions for Sustainable Urban Living* (London: Gaia Books, 1992).

8.   Eugene Linden, "The Exploding Cities of the Developing World," *Foreign Affairs*, January/February 1996; Norman Hammond, "Ancient Cities," *Scientific American*, Special Issue, vol. 5, no. 1 (1994); Robert M. Adams, "The Origin of Cities," *Scientific American*, September 1960 (reprinted in Special Issue, 1994); Lewis Mumford, *The City in History* (San Diego, CA: Harcourt Brace, 1961).

9.   Peter Hall, *Cities in Civilization* (New York: Pantheon Books, 1998).

10.   Fernand Braudel, *Civilization and Capitalism, 15–18th Century, Volume III: the Perspective of the World*, translated from the French by Sian Reynolds (Berkeley, CA: University of California Press, 1992).

11.   Josef Konvitz, *The Urban Millennium: The City-Building Process from the Early Middle Ages to the Present* (Carbondale, IL: Southern Illinois University Press, 1985).

12. James Howard Kunstler, *The Geography of Nowhere* (New York: Touchstone, Simon and Schuster, 1993); Joel Garreau, *Edge City: Life on the New Frontier* (New York: Doubleday, 1991); Kenneth Jackson, *Crabgrass Frontier: The Suburbanization of the United States* (New York: Oxford University Press, 1985); U.S. Department of Commerce, Bureau of the Census, *State and Metropolitan Area Data Book* (Washington, DC: U.S. Government Printing Office, 1997); Wendell Cox Consultancy, "US Urbanized Area: 1950–1990 Data and Ranking Tables," <http://www.publicpurpose.com>, viewed 10 November 1998.

13. U.N., *World Urbanization Prospects: the 1996 Revision*, op. cit. note 2; U.N. Centre for Human Settlements (Habitat), *An Urbanizing World: Global Report on Human Settlements 1996* (Oxford, U.K.: Oxford University Press, 1996).

14. Habitat, op. cit. note 13; Saskia Sassen, "Urban Impacts of Economic Globalization," Comparative Urban Studies Occasional Paper Series No. 5 (Washington, DC: Woodrow Wilson International Center for Scholars, undated); Robert Kaplan, "In the Lexicon of the New Cartography, All Roads Will Lead to City-States," *The World Paper*, July 1998; Robert Kaplan, *An Empire Wilderness* (New York: Random House, 1998).

15. Modern infrastructure from Peter Hall, *Cities of Tomorrow*, updated ed. (Oxford, U.K.: Blackwell Publishers, 1996); Table 1 from Chandler, op. cit. note 3, and U.N., *World Urbanization Prospects: the 1996 Revision*, op. cit. note 2; India from U.N., *World Population Prospects: the 1998 Revision*, op. cit. note 2, and Pravin Visaria, *Urbanization in India: An Overview*, Working Paper No. 52 (Ahmedabad, India: Gujarat Institute of Development Research, September 1993). Urban India would be the fourth most populous nation after China, Rural India, and the United States.

16. Table 2 from U.N., *World Urbanization Prospects*, op. cit. note 2, and Chandler, op. cit. note 3; Figure 1 and map from U.N., *World Urbanization Prospects*, op. cit. note 2.

17. U.N., *World Urbanization Prospects*, op. cit. note 2; John D. Karsada and Allan Parnell, *Third World Cities: Problems, Policies, and Prospects* (Newbury Park, CA: Sage Publications, 1993); "mega-villages" from Martin Brockerhoff and Ellen Brennan, "The Poverty of Cities in Developing Regions," *Population and Development Review*, March 1998.

18. Mumford, op. cit. note 8; Martin Melosi, *Garbage in the Cities* (College Station, TX: Texas A&M Press, 1981); Dickens from James A. Clapp, *The City: A Dictionary of Quotable Thoughts on Cities and Urban Life* (New Brunswick, NJ: Center for Urban Policy Research, Rutgers University, 1987).

19. Nineteenth-century engineers from Hans van Engen, Dietrich Kampe, and Sybrand Tjallingii, eds., *Hydropolis: The Role of Water in Urban Planning* (Leiden, the Netherlands: Backhuys Publishers, 1995); French cities from John Briscoe, "When the Cup's Half Full," *Environment*, May 1993.

20. Mark A. Ridgely, "Water, Sanitation and Resource Mobilization: Expanding the Range of Choices," in G. Shabbir Cheema, ed., *Urban Management: Policies and Innovations in Developing Countries* (Westport, CT: Praeger, 1993); World Health Organization (WHO), *Water Supply and Sanitation Sector Monitoring Report 1996* (Geneva: 1996); WHO, *The World Health Report 1998* (Geneva: 1998); WHO, *The Urban Health Crisis* (Geneva: 1996); WRI, et al., op. cit. note 4.

21. Uncollected trash from Habitat, op. cit. note 13; Mount Smoky from WRI, et al., op. cit. note 4, and from "Smoky Mountain Blues," *The Economist*, 9 September 1995.

22. Developing world from Habitat, op. cit. note 13; waste disposal methods from WHO, *Solid Waste and Health*, Local Authorities, Health and Environment Briefing Pamphlet Series No. 5 (Geneva: 1995).

23. Vitruvius, *Ten Books on Architecture*, cited in van Engen, Kampe, and Tjallingii, op. cit. note 19; Mats Dynesius and Christer Nisson, "Fragmentation and Flow Regulation of River Systems in the Northern Third of the World," *Science*, 4 November 1994.

24. Share of water farmers use and water use since 1900 from Shiklomanov, op. cit. note 6; IFPRI cited in Postel, op. cit. note 6; western United States from "Water in the West: Buying a Gulp of the Colorado," *The Economist*, 24 January 1998, and from Tony Perry, "California and the West: Mediator Will Try to Keep Water War from Boiling Over, *Los Angeles Times*, 6 April 1999; China from "Official Says West Has Duty to Provide Grants, Loans, to Help Fight Water Shortage," *International Environment Reporter*, 29 April 1998, and from Wang Wenyuan, "High Time to Conserve Water Asset," *China Daily*, 20 April 1998; pollution from R.L. Welcomme, "Relationships between Fisheries and the Integrity of River Systems," *Regulated Rivers: Research & Management*, vol. 11, pp. 121–136, 1995.

25. Chester Arnold and James Gibbons, "Impervious Surface Coverage: The Emergence of a Key Environmental Indicator," *Journal of the American Planning Association*, March 1996; Thomas Dunne and Luna B. Leopold, *Water in Environmental Planning* (New York: W.H. Freeman and Company, 1998, 15th ed.).

26. National Research Council, Academica de la Investigacion Cientifica, A.C., Academia Nacional de Ingenieria, A.C., *Mexico City's Water Supply* (Washington, DC: National Academy Press, 1995).

27. Nutrient cycle from Gary Gardner, *Recycling Organic Waste: From Urban Pollutant to Farm Resource*, Worldwatch Paper 135 (Washington, DC: Worldwatch Institute, August 1997); Cairo or Rio from FAO, *The State of Food and Agriculture* (Rome: 1998); New York from Toni Nelson, "Closing the Nutrient Loop," *World Watch*, November/December 1996, and from Vivian Toy, "Planning to Close Its Landfill, New York Will Export Trash," *New York*

Times, 30 November 1996; nitrogen pollution from Peter Vitousek, *Human Alternation of the Global Nitrogen Cycle: Causes and Consequences* (Washington, DC: Ecological Society of America, 1997).

28. Waring cited in Anne Whiston Spirn, *The Granite Garden: Urban Nature and Human Design* (New York: Basic Books, 1984); waste generation from Habitat, op. cit. note 13; Fresh Kills from New York Department of Sanitation, <http://www.ci.nyc.ny.us/html/dos/home.html>, viewed 11 February 1999; waste generation from Habitat, op. cit. note 13.

29. Watershed protection from Todd Wilkinson, "An Upstream Solution to River Pollution," *Christian Science Monitor*, 19 May 1997; New York from Douglas Martin, "Water Projects Cost So Much That Even Environmentalists Worry," *New York Times*, 15 June 1998, and from Geoffrey Ryan, New York City Department of Environmental Protection, discussion with author, 28 October 1998; San José from Richard Gilbert, et al., *Making Cities Work: The Role of Local Authorities in the Urban Environment* (London: Earthscan, 1996).

30. Spirn, op. cit. note 28.

31. Sandra Postel, *Last Oasis* (New York: W.W. Norton & Company, 1997, rev. ed.); Rutherford Platt, "The 2020 Water Supply Study for Metropolitan Boston: The Demise of Diversion," *Journal of the American Planning Association*, March 1995; Jonathan Yeo, Massachusetts Water Resources Authority, Water Works Division, discussion with author, 27 October 1998.

32. Manila and Singapore from Habitat, op. cit. note 13; problem of theft from "The Pipes Aren't Leaking But the Water's Gone," *Urban Age*, winter 1999.

33. Organisation for Economic Co-operation and Development (OECD), *Water Subsidies and the Environment* (Paris: 1997); Bogor from Ismail Serageldin, *Toward Sustainable Management of Water Resources*, Directions in Development (Washington, DC: World Bank, 1995).

34. Ismail Serageldin, *Water Supply, Sanitation, and Environmental Sustainability: The Financing Challenge*, Directions in Development (Washington, DC: World Bank, 1994); Habitat, op. cit. note 13.

35. Tokyo Metropolitan Government, "Action Program for Creating an Eco-Society" (draft), Tokyo, February 1998.

36. Gleick, op. cit. note 6; "Sustainable Water Management Systems Must Be Developed Soon," *International Environment Reporter*, 18 March 1998; Janusz Niemczynowicz, "Megacities from a Water Perspective," *Water International*, vol. 21 (1996); Peter Rogers, Hynd Bouhia, and John Kalbermatten, "Water for Big Cities: Big Problems, Easy Solutions?" paper for the Woodrow Wilson International Center for Scholars' Comparative Urban Studies Project on Urbanization, Population, Security, and the Environment, Washington, DC, 8–9 February 1999.

37. Wetlands treatment in general from Robert Bastian and Jay Benforado, "Waste Treatment: Doing What Comes Naturally," *Technology Review,* February 1983; Arizona from David Rosenbaum, "Wetlands Bloom in the Desert," *Engineering News-Record,* 11 December 1995, and from David Schwartz, "Phoenix Uses Cleaning Power of Wetlands to Scrub Sewage," *Christian Science Monitor,* 16 January 1997.

38. Organic waste from U.S. Environmental Protection Agency, *Organic Materials Management Strategies* (Washington, DC: 1998); industrial countries from OECD, *Environmental Data Compendium 1997* (Paris: 1997); European cities from Josef Barth and Holger Stöppler-Zimmer, "Compost Quality in Europe," *Biocycle,* August 1998.

39. Waste-based industries from Jennifer Ray Beckman, "Recycling-Based Manufacturing Boosts Local Economies in U.S.," *Ecological Economics Bulletin,* Fourth Quarter 1997; recycling in U.S. cities from Institute for Local Self-Reliance, *Cutting the Waste Stream in Half: Community Record-Setters Show How* (draft) (Washington, DC: October 1998).

40. Tokyo from "Tokyo Examines Fees For Collection of Garbage from Households by 1999," *International Environment Reporter,* 5 February 1997; Graz from *First Steps: Local Agenda 21 in Practice* (London: Her Majesty's Stationery Office, 1994) and International Council for Local Environmental Initiatives (ICLEI), "Profiting from Pollution Prevention," case study (Toronto: 1994).

41. Kalundborg from Steven Peck and Chris Callaghan, "Gathering Steam: Eco-Industrial Parks Exchange Waste for Efficiency and Profit," *Alternatives Journal,* spring 1997.

42. U.S. cities from Mark Dwortzan, "The Greening of Industrial Parks," *Technology Review,* 11 January 1998; Chattanooga from Van Henderson, "From Gray to Green: the Story of Chattanooga," *Calypso Log,* February 1995; Dave Flessner, "Tunneling a New Future," *The Chattanooga Times,* 22 July 1998.

43. Arif Hasan, "Replicating the Low-Cost Sanitation Programme Administered by the Orangi Pilot Project in Karachi, Pakistan," in Ismail Serageldin, Michael Cohen, and K.C. Sivaramakrishnan, eds. *The Human Face of the Urban Environment,* Proceedings of the Second Annual World Bank Conference on Environmentally Sustainable Development (Washington, DC: World Bank, 1995); Fred Pearce, "Squatters Take Control," *New Scientist,* 1 June 1996; Akhtar Badshah, *Our Urban Future* (London: Zed Books, 1996).

44. Susan Hall, "Lessons from a Semi-Private Enterprise in Bandung, Indonesia," in U.S. Agency for International Development (USAID), *Privatizing Solid Waste Management Services in Developing Countries,* Proceedings Paper (Washington, DC: International City/County Management Association, 1992); ICLEI, "Bandung, Indonesia: Solid Waste Management,"

Project Summary 67 (Toronto: 1991); Badshah, op. cit. note 43.

45. John Young and Aaron Sachs, *The Next Efficiency Revolution: Creating a Sustainable Materials Economy*, Worldwatch Paper 121 (Washington, DC: Worldwatch Institute, September 1994); Herbert Muschamp, "Greening a South Bronx Brownfield," *New York Times*, 23 January 1998; Lis Harris, "Annals of the South Bronx: Banana Kelly's Toughest Fight," *New Yorker*, 24 July 1995; Allen Hershkowitz, Natural Resources Defense Council, discussion with author, 27 April 1999.

46. Funds needed for reliable water systems from Serageldin, op. cit. note 25; $1 trillion from Rogers et al., op. cit. note 36.

47. United Kingdom and France from David Suratgar, "World Water: Financing the Future," *The Journal of Project Finance*, summer 1998, and from Frederico Neto, "Water Privatization and Regulation in England and France: A Tale of Two Models," *Natural Resources Forum*, May 1998; percentage from private sources from Bradford Gentry and Lisa Fernandez, "Evolving Public-Private Partnerships: General Themes and Examples from the Urban Water Sector," *Globalisation and the Environment: Perspectives from OECD and Dynamic Non-Member Economies*, OECD Proceedings (Paris: OECD, 1998); privatization trend from Gisele Silva, Nicola Tynan, and Yesim Yilmaz, "Private Participation in the Water and Sewerage Sector—Recent Trends," *Private Sector*, September 1998; Buenos Aires from Emmanuel Ideolvitch and Klas Ringskog, *Private Sector Participation in Water Supply and Sanitation in Latin America*, Directions in Development (Washington, DC: World Bank, 1995).

48. David Haarmeyer and Ashoka Mody, "Private Capital in Water and Sanitation," *Finance and Development*, March 1997; Penelope J. Brook Cowen, "Bail Out: The Global Privatization of Water Supply," *Urban Age*, winter 1999.

49. UNDP, *Urban Agriculture: Food, Jobs and Sustainable Cities* (New York: 1996); Luc J.A. Mougeot, "Farming Inside and Around Cities," *Urban Age*, winter 1998; Jane Jacobs, *The Economy of Cities* (New York: Random House, 1969).

50. David Morris, *Self-Reliant Cities: Energy and the Transformation of Urban America* (San Francisco: Sierra Club Books, 1982).

51. Girardet, op. cit. note 7.

52. U.K. supermarkets from Margaret Bergen, "The Challenge to Wholesale Markets," *Urban Age*, winter 1998; size of average generator is a Worldwatch estimate based on U.S. Department of Energy, Energy Information Administration, *Annual Electric Generator Report*, electronic database (Washington, DC: 1993).

53. Wuppertal Institute, *Road Transport of Goods and the Effects on the Spatial*

Environment, 1993, cited in Richard Douthwaite, *Short Circuit: Strengthening Local Economies for Security in an Unstable World* (Devon, U.K.: Green Books, 1996).

54. Crop uniformity from Stephen R. Gliessman, *Agroecology: Ecological Processes in Sustainable Agriculture* (Chelsea, MI: Ann Arbor Press, 1998) and John Tuxill, "Appreciating the Benefits of Plant Biodiversity," in Lester Brown et al., *State of the World 1999* (New York: W.W. Norton & Company, 1999); acidification from Gywneth Howells, *Acid Rain and Acid Waters*, (London: Ellis Horwood Limited, 2nd ed., 1995); carbon from Houghton et al., op. cit. note 6; hungry people from FAO, *The State of Food and Agriculture 1998* (Rome: 1998); people without electricity from World Bank, *Rural Energy and Development: Improving Energy Supplies for Two Billion People* (Washington, DC: 1996).

55. Gliessman, op. cit. note 54; Michael Shuman, *Going Local: Creating Self-Reliant Communities in a Global Age* (New York: The Free Press, 1998); Jim Pierro, *Orion Afield*, summer 1998; dollar value from UNDP, op. cit. note 49, and Ralph Heimlich, "Agriculture Adapts to Urbanization," *Food Review*, U.S. Department of Agriculture, January 1991.

56. UNDP, op. cit. note 49.

57. F.H. King, *Farmers of Forty Centuries: On Permanent Agriculture in China, Korea and Japan* (Emmaus, PA: Organic Gardening Press, 1947); UNDP, op. cit. note 49.

58. Diana Lee-Smith, "Time to Help the City Farmers of Africa," *People and the Planet*, vol. 5, no. 2 (1996); Nelson, op. cit. note 27; UNDP, op. cit. note 49.

59. Gliessman, op. cit. note 54.

60. UNDP, op. cit. note 49.

61. Ibid.

62. Ibid; Curitiba from Jonas Rabinovitch and Josef Leitmann, Environmental Innovation and Management in Curitiba, Brazil, UMP Working Paper No. 1 (Washington, DC: UNDP/Habitat/World Bank, 1993).

63. Mougeot, op. cit. note 49; Mariana Rodriguez, "Street Youth Become Urban Farmers in Rosario, Argentina and Vancouver, Canada," *Alternatives Journal*, summer 1998; Ann Scott Tyson, "Urban Farms: How Green Is My Barrio," *Christian Science Monitor*, 4 December 1996; H. Patricia Hynes, *A Patch of Eden: America's Inner-City Gardeners* (White River Junction, VT: Chelsea Green Publishing Company, 1996).

64. Solar panels from Paul Maycock, *PV News*, various issues; SMUD from

Sacramento Municipal Utility District (SMUD), "PV Pioneer Program," <http://www.smud.org/energy/solar/index.html>, viewed 16 December 1997, and from Robert Masullo, "SMUD Solar Programs Signal Dawning of Next Age in Electricity," *Sacramento Bee*, 5 October 1997; SMUD estimate from Don Osborne, SMUD, Sacramento, CA; interview with author, 17 July 1998; geothermal from Laurent Belsie, "The Time Has Come for Geothermal Heat Pumps," *Christian Science Monitor*, 30 July 1996; Andrew Revkin, "Two Deepest Holes in Town Will Bring Heat Back Up," *New York Times*, April 20, 1997; Paul C. Liepe, "GeoExchange Systems Heat and Cool Commercial Buildings," *Environmental Design and Construction*, January/February 1998; natural gas turbines from Thomas R. Casten, *Turning Off the Heat* (Amherst, NY: Prometheus Books, 1998), and from Gerard Cler and Nicholas Lenssen, *Distributed Generation; Markets and Technologies in Transition* (Boulder, CO: E-Source, December 1997).

65. ICLEI, *Local Government Implementation of Climate Protection: Case Studies* (Toronto: 1997).

66. Turkey from Cetin Goksu, "Toward Solar Towns," *Ekistics: The Problems and Science of Human Settlements*, double issue, May/June–July/August 1994; David Malin Roodman and Nicholas Lenssen, *A Building Revolution: How Ecology and Health Concerns Are Transforming Construction*, Worldwatch Paper 124 (Washington, DC: Worldwatch Institute, March 1995); Toronto from ICLEI, op. cit. note 65.

67. Brad Horn, "Landscaping Gets Back to Nature," *Environmental Design and Construction*, June 1998; Chicago from E. Gregory McPherson, David J. Nowak, and Rowan A. Rowntree, *Chicago's Urban Forest Ecosystem: Results of the Chicago Urban Forest Climate Project* (Radnor, PA: Northeastern Forest Experiment Station, Forest Service, U.S. Department of Agriculture, June 1994); Eco-roofs from J. William Thompson, "Grass-Roofs Movement," *Landscape Architecture*, May 1998; Malaysia from Dwight Holing, "Sustainable Skyscrapers," *Tomorrow*, October–December 1995.

68. ICLEI, op. cit. note 65.

69. Barriers from Casten, op. cit. note 64; solar from Christopher Flavin and Molly O'Meara, "Solar Power Markets Boom," *World Watch*, September/October 1998.

70. Milwaukee from American Forests, *The State of the Urban Forest: Assessing Tree Cover and Developing Goals* (Washington, DC: September 1997), <http://www.americanforests.org/ufc/uea/stateof.html>, viewed 29 April 1999; connection with nature from John F. Dwyer, Herbert Schroeder, and Paul Gobster, "The Deep Significance of Urban Trees and Forests," in Rutherford H. Platt, Rowan A. Rowntree, and Pamela C. Muick, eds., *The Ecological City* (Amherst, MA: University of Massachusetts Press, 1994); patients from Roger S. Ulrich, "View Through a Window May Influence Recovery from Surgery," *Science*, 27 April 1984.

71. Morris, op. cit. note 50.

72. Marcia Lowe, *Shaping Cities: The Environmental and Human Dimensions,* Worldwatch Paper 105 (Washington, DC: Worldwatch Institute, October 1991); Peter Newman and Jeff Kenworthy, *Sustainability and Cities: Overcoming Automobile Dependence* (Washington, DC: Island Press, 1999).

73. Glenn Yaro, *The Decline of Transit: Urban Transportation in German and U.S. Cities 1900–1970* (Cambridge, U.K.: Cambridge University Press, 1984).

74. Ebenezer Howard, *Garden Cities of Tomorrow* (1902), cited in Robert Fishman, *Urban Utopias in the Twentieth Century* (New York: Basic Books, 1977); Le Corbusier, *The City of Tomorrow and Its Planning,* translated from the 8th French Edition of *Urbanisme* (1924) by Frederick Etchells (Cambridge, MA: MIT Press, 1971).

75. U.S. suburbs from Kunstler, op. cit. note 12; Le Corbusier, op. cit. note 74.

76. Figure 2 based on Newman and Kenworthy, op cit. note 72. U.S. cities are Boston, Chicago, Denver, Detroit, Houston, Los Angeles, New York, Phoenix, San Francisco, and Washington; Australian cities are Adelaide, Brisbane, Melbourne, Perth, and Sydney; Canadian cities are Calgary, Montreal, Ottawa, Toronto, Vancouver, and Winnipeg; Western European cities are Amsterdam, Brussels, Copenhagen, Frankfurt, Hamburg, London, Munich, Paris, Stockholm, Vienna, and Zurich; industrial Asian cities are Hong Kong, Tokyo, and Singapore; and developing Asian cities are Jakarta, Kuala Lumpur, Manila, and Surabaya.

77. Marc L. Imhoff, David Stutzer, William Lawrence, and Christopher Elvidge, "Assessing the Impact of Urban Sprawl on Soil Resources in the United States Using Nighttime 'City Lights' Satellite Images and Digital Soils Maps," in Thomas D. Sisk, ed., *Perspectives on the Land Use History of North America: A Context for Understanding Our Changing Environment,* USGS/BRD/BSR-1998-0003 (Reston, VA: United States Geological Survey, 1998).

78. U.S. estimate is for 1982–92 and is from American Farmland Trust, *Farming on the Edge* (Washington, DC: March 1997); China estimate is for 1991–96 and is from Liu Yinglang, "Legislation to Protect Arable Land," *China Daily,* 15 September 1998; Bangkok from Malcolm Falkus, "Bangkok: From Primate City to Primate Megalopolis," in Theo Barker and Anthony Sutcliffe, eds., *Megalopolis: The Giant City in History* (London: St. Martin's Press, 1993), and from Newman and Kenworthy, op. cit. note 72.

79. Streets from Jane Jacobs, *The Death and Life of Great American Cities* (New York: Random House, 1961), and from Peter Calthorpe, *The Next American Metropolis: Ecology, Community, and the American Dream* (New York: Princeton Architectural Press, 1993); Platt et al., op. cit. note 70, and from Michael Hough, *Cities and Natural Process* (London: Routledge, 1995); São

Paulo from Raquel Rolnick, "Territorial Exclusion and Violence: The Case of São Paulo, Brazil," paper for the Woodrow Wilson International Center for Scholars' Comparative Urban Studies Project on Urbanization, Population, Security, and the Environment, Washington, DC, 14–15 September 1998; Jacobs, op. cit. this note.

80. Jane Holtz Kay, *Asphalt Nation* (New York: Random House, 1997); Annalyn Lacombe and William Lyons, "The Transportation System's Role in Moving Welfare Recipients to Jobs," *Volpe Transportation Journal*, spring 1998; Michael Replogle and Walter Hook, "Improving Access for the Poor in Urban Areas," *Race, Poverty and the Environment*, fall 1995.

81. Worldwide traffic accidents from WHO, *The World Health Report 1995: Bridging the Gaps* (Geneva: 1995); see also Gui Nei, "Traffic Accidents Soaring," *China Daily*, 10 November 1998; Jane Seymour, "Trafficking in Death," *New Scientist*, 14 September 1996; Eduardo A. Vasconcellos, "Transport and Environment in Developing Countries: Comparing Air Pollution and Traffic Accidents as Policy Priorities," *Habitat International*, vol. 21, no. 1 (1997); Matthew Wald, "Pedestrian Death Risk Is Seen as Major Public Health Crisis," *New York Times*, 9 April 1997; Table 3 from Newman and Kenworthy, op. cit. note 72. For Table 3, cities are those listed in note 76 for Figure 2 plus the following additions: for the U.S.: Portland, Sacramento, and San Diego; for Australia: Canberra; for Canada: Edmonton; for developing Asia: Bangkok, Beijing, and Seoul.

82. Deaths from WHO, *The World Health Report 1997* (Geneva: 1997); traffic pollution from from D. Schwela and O. Zali, eds., *Urban Traffic Pollution* (New York: Routledge, 1999); Peter Gaupp, "Air Pollution in the Third World," *Swiss Review of World Affairs*, February 1997; Utpal Chatterjee, "Expert Paints Gloomy Picture of Pollution," *The Times of India*, 27 April 1998; Anju Sharma and Anumita Roychowdhury, *Slow Murder: The Deadly Story of Vehicular Pollution in India* (New Delhi: Centre for Science and Environment, 1996); ozone levels from WHO, "WHO Guidelines for Air Quality," Fact Sheet No. 187 (Geneva: December 1997); Molly Moore, "Mexico City Gasping in Quest of Fair Air," *Washington Post*, 25 November 1996; Anthony Faiola, "Santiago's Children Gasp for Cleaner Air," *Washington Post*, 12 July 1998; lead in gasoline from WRI et al., *World Resources 1998–99* (New York: Oxford University Press, 1998); toxic effects of lead from Jack Hollander, ed., *The Energy-Environment Connection* (Washington, DC: Island Press, 1992); Delhi from "Delhi Children Have High Level of Lead in Blood," *The Statesman* (India), 9 July 1998; Chanda Handa, "Umbilical Discord," *Down to Earth*, 31 May 1998; Shanghai from X.M. Shen et al., "Childhood Lead Poisoning in Children," *Science of the Total Environment*, vol. 181, 1996, cited in World Bank, *Clear Water, Blue Skies: China's Environment in the New Century* (Washington, DC: 1997); Cairo from Howard Schneider, "Colossal Gridlock on the Nile," *Washington Post*, 20 January 1999; "36 Stations Monitor Lead Pollution in Cairo," *Agence France Presse*, 28 January 1999.

83. Walter Hook and Michael Replogle, "Motorization and Non-Motorized Transport in Asia," *Land Use Policy*, vol. 13, no. 1 (1996); Graham Haughton and Colin Hunter, *Sustainable Cities*, Regional Policy and Development Series 7 (London: Jessica Kingsley Publishers, 1994); Arnold and Gibbons, op. ct. note 25.

84. Transportation from Newman and Kenworthy, op. cit. note 72; buildings' materials and energy use from Roodman and Lenssen, op. cit. note 4; Minneapolis and St. Paul from Myron Orfield, *Metropolitics* (Washington, DC: Brookings Institution, 1997).

85. Jeff Kenworthy et al., *Indicators of Transport Efficiency in 37 Global Cities* (Washington, DC: World Bank, 1997); PriceWaterhouse Coopers Lend Lease Ratings cited in Neal Peirce, "Investment Market Message to Atlanta: Grow Smarter," *Sacramento Bee*, 3 January 1999; Bell South executive from Noah Adams, "All Things Considered," National Public Radio, 10 May 1999; U.S. hours in traffic from Texas Transportation Institute, *Mobility Study*, summary at <http://www.mobility.tamu.edu/study/>, viewed 24 August 1998; investment in road construction from Surface Transportation Policy Project, *An Analysis of the Relationship Between Highway Expansion and Congestion in Metropolitan Areas: Lessons from the 15-year Texas Transportation Institute Study* (Washington, DC: 1998), at <http://www.transact.org>, and Alan Sipress, "Widen the Roads, Drivers Will Come," *Washington Post*, 4 January 1999.

86. Michael Wals and Jitendra Shah, *Clean Fuels for Asia*, World Bank Technical Paper No. 377 (Washington, DC: World Bank, 1997); Jitendra Shah and Tanvi Nagpal, eds., *Urban Air Quality Management Strategy in Asia: Metro Manila Report*, World Bank Technical Paper No. 380 (Washington, DC: World Bank, 1997).

87. Jonas Rabinovitch and Josef Leitman, "Urban Planning in Curitiba," *Scientific American*, March 1996; Jonas Rabinovitch, "Innovative Land Use and Public Transport Policy," *Land Use Policy*, vol. 13, no. 1 (1996).

88. 30–60 percent from Jorge E. Hardoy and David Satterthwaite, *Squatter Citizen: Life in the Urban Third World* (London: Earthscan, 1989); Curitiba from Bill McKibben, *Hope: Human and Wild* (Boston: Little, Brown and Company, 1995).

89. Netherlands Ministry of Housing, Physical Planning and the Environment, *Fourth Report (EXTRA) on Physical Planning in the Netherlands: Comprehensive Summary, On the Road to 2015* (The Hague: 1991); Dutch master plan from Transportation Research Board, Washington, DC, 13 January 1999; rates of bicycle use from Newman and Kenworthy, op. cit. note 72, and from Gary Gardner, "When Cities Take Bicycles Seriously," *World Watch*, September/October 1998; Sweden from Newman and Kenworthy, op. cit. note 72, and from Michael Bernick and Robert Cervero, *Transit Villages in the 21st Century* (New York: McGraw-Hill, 1997).

90. Richard Moe and Carter Wilkie, *Changing Places: Rebuilding Community in the Age of Sprawl* (New York: Henry Holt, 1997); Alan Thein Durning, *The Car and the City* (Seattle, WA: Northwest Environment Watch, 1996); Mike Burton, Portland Metro Chief, Portland, OR, discussion with author, 18 June 1998.

91. Philip Langdon and Corby Kummer, "How Portland Does It: A City That Protects its Thriving Civil Core," *The Atlantic Monthly*, November 1992; Newman and Kenworthy, op. cit. note 72.

92. Peter Calthorpe, *The Next American Metropolis: Ecology Community and the American Dream* (New York: Princeton Architectural Press, 1993); James Howard Kunstler, *Home from Nowhere: Remaking our Everyday World for the 21st Century* (New York: Simon and Schuster, 1996); Phyllis Myers' report for the Brookings Institution, "Livability at the Ballot Box: State and Local Referenda on Parks, Conservation, and Smarter Growth, Election Day 1998," <http://www.srsmyers.org>, viewed 10 March 1999.

93. H. William Batt, "Motor Vehicle Transportation and Proper Pricing: User Fees, Environmental Fees, and Value Capture," *Ecological Economics Bulletin*, first quarter 1998; David Weller, "For Whom the Road Tolls: Road Pricing in Singapore," *Harvard International Review*, summer 1998; Donald Shoup, "Congress Okays Cash Out," *Access*, fall 1998; Todd Litman, "The Costs of Automobile Dependency" (Victoria, BC, Canada: Victoria Transport Policy Institute, 1996).

94. Todd Litman, "The Costs of Automobile Dependency" (Victoria, BC, Canada: Victoria Transport Policy Institute, 1996); Mary Williams Walsh, "Instant Mobility, No Headaches," *The Sun*, 3 August 1998; European Academy of the Urban Environment, "Berlin: Stattauto-Germany Largest Car-Sharing Company," *SURBAN-Good Practice in Urban Development* electronic database (Berlin: June 1997). The SURBAN database is available at <http://www.eaue.de/>. European Car Sharing, <http://www.carsharing.org>, viewed 27 May 1999; Susanna Jacona Salafia, "Italy Shares Electric Cars to Cut Emissions," *Environmental News Service*, 11 December 1998.

95. David Malin Roodman, *The Natural Wealth of Nations* (New York: W.W. Norton & Company, 1998); Alan Thein Durning and Yoram Bauman, *Tax Shift* (Seattle, WA: Northwest Environment Watch, 1998).

96. Durning and Bauman, op. cit. note 95.

97. Roodman, op. cit. note 95.

98. Preservation programs from "The Varied Landscape of Park and Conservation Finance," *Greensense*, spring 1997; Maryland from Peter S. Goodman, "Glendening vs. Suburban Sprawl," *Washington Post*, 6 October 1998, and Maryland Department of Natural Resources, "Maryland's Smart Growth Initiative, <http://www.dnr.state.md.us>, viewed 20 May 1999.

99. Anne Spackman, "The Pressure is on for a Brown Future," *Financial Times*, 13–14 June 1998; Thomas K. Wright and Ann Davlin, "Overcoming Obstacles to Brownfield and Vacant Land Redevelopment," *Land Lines*, Newsletter of the Lincoln Institute of Land Policy, Cambridge, MA, September 1998; Wes Sanders, "Environmental Justice, Urban Revitalization, and Brownfields," *Orion Afield*, spring 1998; "EPA Awards Grants to 17 More Brownfields Projects in Midwest," *PR Newswire*, 15 July 1998; U.S. Environmental Protection Agency, "Brownfields Pilots," <http://www.epa.gov/swerosps/bf/pilot.htm>, viewed 25 May 1999.

100. Don Chen, STPP, Washington, DC, presentation at Transportation Research Board annual meeting, January 1999; James K. Hoeveler, "Accessibility vs. Mobility: The Location Efficient Mortgage," Center for Neighborhood Technology, <http://links.cnt.org/lem/>, viewed 1 April 1999; James K. Hoeveler, Center for Neighborhood Technology, Chicago, IL, discussion with author, 27 April 1999.

101. Urban rail from Chris Bushell, ed., *Jane's Urban Transport Systems, 1995–96* (Surrey, U.K.: Jane's Information Group, 1995); Curitiba from Rabinovitch and Leitman, op. cit. note 87; Copenhagen from ICLEI, *Initiatives Newsletter,* November 1997, and Gardner, op. cit. note 89.

102. Kevin Shafizadeh, Debbie Niemeier, Patricia Mokhtarian, and Ilan Salomon, "The Costs and Benefits of Telecommuting: An Evaluation of Macro-Scale Literature (Davis, CA: Partners for Advanced Transit and Highways, July 1997); Management Technology Associates 1994, *Telework-Based Transport Telecommunications Substitution 1993–94*, Report of the Department of Transport, cited in Duncan McLaren, Simon Bullock, and Nusrat Yousuf, *Tomorrow's World: Britain's Share in a Sustainable Future* (London: Earthscan, 1998).

103. Tom Standage, *The Victorian Internet: The Remarkable Story of the Telegraph and the Nineteenth Century's On-Line Pioneers* (New York: Walker and Company, 1998); William J. Mitchell, *City of Bits: Space, Place, and the Infobahn* (Cambridge, MA: MIT Press, 1995); Peter Hall, *Cities in Civilization* (New York: Pantheon Books, 1998); Henton quoted in Neal Peirce, "The New Workplace," *Urban Age*, autumn 1998; Adobe from Adams, op. cit. note 85.

104. Mesopotamia from Heather Pringle, "Cradle of Cash," *Discover*, October 1998; disproportionate share from World Bank, "A Strategic View of Urban and Local Government Issues: Implications for the Bank," draft strategy paper, May 1999.

105. Devolution of responsibility from Habitat, op. cit. note 13, and David Perry, ed., *Building the Public City: The Politics, Governance, and Finance of Public Infrastructure* (Thousand Oaks, CA: Sage Publications, 1995); Roy Bahl and Johannes Linn, *Urban Public Finance in Developing Countries* (New York: Oxford University Press for the International Bank for

Reconstruction and Development, 1992).

106. Perverse incentives from Habitat, op. cit. note 13.

107. U.S. reforms from F. Kaid Benfield, Matthew D. Raimi, and Donald D.T. Chen, *Once There Were Greenfields: How Urban Sprawl is Undermining America's Environment, Economy and Social Fabric* (New York: Natural Resources Defense Council, 1999); Japan from Paul Maycock, "Japan Expands '70000 Roofs' Program, *PV News*, July 1998.

108. Bahl and Linn, op. cit. note 105; Figure 3 from Urban Indicators Programme, Global Urban Observatory, U.N. Centre for Human Settlements, Global Urban Indicators Database (Nairobi: 1998): <http://www.urbanobservatory.org>, viewed 20 August 1998.

109. George Peterson, "What Kind of Financing Systems Support Decentralization?" *The Urban Age*, September 1995; Harry Kitchen, "Pricing of Local Government Services," in Paul A.R. Hobson and France St-Hilaire, eds., *Urban Governance and Finance: A Question of Who Does What* (Montreal: Institute for Research on Public Policy, 1997).

110. Roodman, op. cit. note 95.

111. Akin Mabogunje, "Preparing African Cities for the Bond Market," *Urban Age*, spring 1998; "The Varied Landscape of Park and Conservation Finance," op. cit. note 98; Kim Hopper, *Increasing Public Investment in Parks and Open Space: Local Parks, Local Financing—Volume I* (San Francisco: Trust for Public Land, 1998).

112. "The Varied Landscape of Park and Conservation Finance," op. cit. note 98.

113. Philip Gidman with Ian Blore, Jens Lorentzen, and Paul Schuttenbelt, *Public-Private Partnerships in Urban Infrastructure Services*, UMP Working Paper No. 4 (Nairobi: UNDP/UNCHS (Habitat)/World Bank, 1995); Timothy Irwin, "Responsible Investing for Cities and Taxpayers," *Urban Age*, vol. 5, no. 2 (1997); Ismail Serageldin, Richard Barrett, and Joan Martin-Brown, eds., *The Business of Sustainable Cities: Public-Private Partnerships for Creative Technical and Institutional Solutions*, Environmentally Sustainable Development Proceedings Series No. 7 (Washington, DC: World Bank, 1995); survey of mayors from UNDP, "Urban Problems Remain Similar Worldwide," press release (New York: 28 July 1997); UNDP from "Public-Private Partnerships for the Urban Environment," <http://www.undp.org/>, viewed 26 October 1998.

114. Nineteenth century from World Bank, *World Development Report 1994* (New York: Oxford University Press, 1994); Asian financial crisis from Andrew Pollack, "Asia Drop Sends Shivers Through Builders," *New York Times*, 2 November 1997; Tessa Tennant, "Infrastructure Plans on Hold,"

Tomorrow, January/February 1998; World Bank, *Global Economic Prospects and the Developing Countries; 1998/9* (Washington, DC: 1999); and stadiums from Mark Bernstein, "Sports Stadium Boondoogle," *The Public Interest,* 22 June 1998; and from David Morris and Daniel Kraker, "Rooting the Home Team: Why the Packers Won't Leave—and Why the Browns Did," *The American Prospect,* September/October 1998.

115. Dinesh Mehta, "Participatory Urban Environmental Management: A Case of Ahmedabad, India," paper for the Woodrow Wilson International Center for Scholars' Comparative Urban Studies Project on Urbanization, Population, Security, and the Environment, Washington, DC, 14–15 September 1998; Jonathan Karp, "Muni Bonds Become Novel Way of Funding City Projects in India," *Wall Street Journal,* 26 November 1997; Patralekha Chatterjee, "India ULBs Give Lenders More than IOUs," *Urban Age,* vol. 5, no. 2 (1997); Priscilla Phelps, ed., *Municipal Bond Market Development in Developing Countries: The Experience of the U.S. Agency for International Development* (Washington, DC: USAID Finance Working Paper, November 1997).

116. Community enterprise zones from Barry Rubin, "Enterprise Zones: Cure for Urban Ills," *Forum for Applied Research and Public Policy,* winter 1995; Michael Porter, *On Competition* (Boston, MA: Harvard Business School Publishing, 1996).

117. Gary Stix, "Small (Lending) is Beautiful," *Scientific American,* April 1997; Ismail Serageldin, "Helping Out with Tiny Loans," *Journal of Commerce,* 2 April 1997; Maria Otero and Elisabeth Rhyne, *The New World of Microenterprise Finance: Building Healthy Financial Institutions for the Poor* (West Hartford, CT: Kumarian Press, 1994); Mary McNeil, "Access to Credit for the Poor: Adapting the Grameen Bank Model to Urban Areas," Infrastructure Notes, Transportation, Water, and Urban Development Department, World Bank, November 1992; Douthwaite, op. cit. note 53.

118. OECD, *The Ecological City: Innovative Policies for Sustainable Urban Development* (Paris: 1996).

119. 1000 Friends of Oregon, *Making the Connections: A Summary of the LUTRAQ Project* (Portland, OR: 1997); Molly O'Meara, "How Mid-Size Cities Can Avoid Strangulation," *World Watch,* September/October 1998.

120. 1998 elections from Myers, op. cit. note 92; Earl Blumenauer, U.S. Congress, remarks at National Press Club, 24 March 1999.

121. Carl Bartone, Janis Bernstein, Josef Leitmann, Jochen Eigen, *Toward Environmental Strategies for Cities: Policies for Urban Environmental Management in Developing Countries,* UMP Discussion Paper 18 (Washington, DC: UNDP/Habitat/World Bank, 1994).

122. Josef Leitman, *Rapid Urban Environmental Assessment: Lessons from Cities in the Developing World, Volume 1. Methodology and Preliminary Findings,* UMP

Discussion Paper 14 (Washington, DC: UNDP/Habitat/World Bank, 1994); Habitat II from Eric Carlson, "The Legacy of Habitat II," *The Urban Age*, August 1996, and from U.N., *Report of the U.N. Conference on Human Settlements (Habitat II)*, Istanbul, 3–14 June 1996; ICLEI, in cooperation with the U.N. Department for Policy Coordination and Sustainable Development, *Local Agenda 21 Survey* (New York: March 1997).

123. Leitman, op. cit. note 122; Jay Moor, Global Urban Observatory, e-mail to author, 16 October 1998; Christine Auclir, "Researchers Needed for Global Urban Database," *Urban Age*, spring 1998.

124. Elizabeth Kline, "Sustainable Community Indicators: How to Measure Progress," in Mark Roseland, ed., *Eco-City Dimensions: Healthy Communities, Healthy Planet* (Gabriola Island, BC, Canada: New Society Publishers, 1997); Donella Meadows, *Indicators and Information Systems for Sustainable Development: A Report to the Balaton Group* (Hartland Four Corners, VT: Sustainability Institute, 1998).

125. Zhang Feng, "Residents Active in Fighting Pollution," *China Daily* 28 December 1998; Elisabeth Rosenthal, "China Officially Lifts Filter on Staggering Pollution Data," *New York Times*, 14 June 1998; Samuel Paul, "Report Cards: A Novel Approach for Improving Urban Services," *Urban Age*, January 1996.

126. John Wilson, "Reinventing Local Government with GIS," *Public Works*, May 1995; Charles Moore, "When GIS Comes to the Neighborhood," *Planning*, July 1998; location-efficient mortgages from Hoeveler, op. cit. note 100; Quito from Roman Pryjomko and Peter Rabley, "Mapping the Future," *Urban Age*, autumn 1998.

127. Buenos Aires from David Wheeler, "Information in Pollution Management: The New Model," in *Brazil: Managing Pollution Problems, The Brown Environmental Agenda* (Washington, DC: World Bank, June 1997), <http://www.worldbank.org/nipr>, viewed 1 April 1999.

128. Minnesota from Orfield, op. cit. note 84; Maryland from Timothy W. Foresman, "The Baltimore-Washington Regional Collaboratory Land-Use History Research Program," in Sisk, ed., op. cit. note 77, and "Baltimore-Washington Regional Collaboratory Overview," <http://umbc7.umbc.edu/bwrdc/projover.html>, viewed 19 April 1999.

129. ICLEI from Richard Gilbert, et al., *Making Cities Work: The Role of Local Authorities in the Urban Environment* (London: Earthscan, 1996); Local Agenda 21's from ICLEI, Toronto, Canada, discussion with author, 17 August 1998; Habitat, "Urban Problems Mushrooming—First Ever Database of Urban Solutions Created," press release (Nairobi: 20 November 1995); Habitat, "Database of Human Settlements: Best Practices Released," press release (Nairobi: 5 October 1998). The database is available at <http:/www.bestpractices.org/>.

130. Mega-Cities Project Inc., *Environmental Innovations for Sustainable Mega-Cities: Sharing Approaches That Work* (New York: 1996); Janice Perlman, "Mega-Cities: Global Urbanization and Innovation," in Cheema, op. cit. note 20; Badshah, op. cit. note 43; Costa Rica from Gilbert, op. cit. note 29.

131. Ayse Kudat, "Urban Environmental Audits: Networking and Participation in Six Mediterranean Cities," in Serageldin, et al., op. cit. note 43.

132. European Commission, *European Sustainable Cities* (Brussels: 1996); WHO Regional Office for Europe, *City Planning for Health and Sustainable Development*, European Sustainable Development and Health Series: 2 (Copenhagen: 1997); Energy-Cités from Gerard Magnin, "The Fourfold Role of Cities in the Industrialized World," *Ecodecision*, autumn 1997.

133. ICLEI, *Local Government Implementation of Climate Protection: Report to the U.N. Conference of the Parties* (Toronto: December 1997); ICLEI and the United States Environmental Protection Agency, *Saving the Climate—Saving the Cities* (Toronto: ICLEI, undated); number of cities in campaign from Tanya Imola, ICLEI, Toronto, discussion with author, 27 April 1999; emissions reductions from ICLEI, op. cit. note 65.

134. Paul Lewis, *Shaping Suburbia: How Political Institutions Organize Urban Development* (Pittsburgh, PA: University of Pittsburgh Press, 1996); Joseph Subiros, *Space and Culture in Washington, DC: A Capital in Search of a City*, Woodrow Wilson International Center for Scholars Comparative Urban Studies Occasional Paper Series, Number 9 (Washington, DC: undated).

135. Bruce Katz and Scott Bernstein, "The New Metropolitan Agenda: Connecting Cities and Suburbs," *The Brookings Review*, fall 1998; David Rusk, *Cities Without Suburbs* (Washington, DC: Woodrow Wilson Center Press, 1993); David Rusk, "The Exploding Metropolis: Why Growth Management Makes Sense," *The Brookings Review*, fall 1998; Orfield, op. cit. note 84.

136. Rabinovitch and Leitmann, op. cit. note 62; Jonas Rabinovitch, UNDP, discussion with author, June 1998.

Worldwatch Papers

No. of Copies

_____147. **Reinventing Cities for People and the Planet** by Molly O'Meara

_____146. **Ending Violent Conflict** by Michael Renner

_____145. **Safeguarding The Health of Oceans** by Anne Platt McGinn

_____144. **Mind Over Matter: Recasting the Role of Materials in Our Lives** by Gary Gardner and Payal Sampat

_____143. **Beyond Malthus: Sixteen Dimensions of the Population Problem** by Lester R. Brown, Gary Gardner, and Brian Halweil

_____142. **Rocking the Boat: Conserving Fisheries and Protecting Jobs** by Anne Platt McGinn

_____141. **Losing Strands in the Web of Life: Vertebrate Declines and the Conservation of Biological Diversity** by John Tuxill

_____140. **Taking a Stand: Cultivating a New Relationship with the World's Forests** by Janet N. Abramovitz

_____139. **Investing in the Future: Harnessing Private Capital Flows for Environmentally Sustainable Development** by Hilary F. French

_____138. **Rising Sun, Gathering Winds: Policies to Stabilize the Climate and Strengthen Economies** by Christopher Flavin and Seth Dunn

_____137. **Small Arms, Big Impact: The Next Challenge of Disarmament** by Michael Renner

_____136. **The Agricultural Link: How Environmental Deterioration Could Disrupt Economic Progress** by Lester R. Brown

_____135. **Recycling Organic Waste: From Urban Pollutant to Farm Resource** by Gary Gardner

_____134. **Getting the Signals Right: Tax Reform to Protect the Environment and the Economy** by David Malin Roodman

_____133. **Paying the Piper: Subsidies, Politics, and the Environment** by David Malin Roodman

_____132. **Dividing the Waters: Food Security, Ecosystem Health, and the New Politics of Scarcity** by Sandra Postel

_____131. **Shrinking Fields: Cropland Loss in a World of Eight Billion** by Gary Gardner

_____130. **Climate of Hope: New Strategies for Stabilizing the World's Atmosphere** by Christopher Flavin and Odil Tunali

_____129. **Infecting Ourselves: How Environmental and Social Disruptions Trigger Disease** by Anne E. Platt

_____128. **Imperiled Waters, Impoverished Future: The Decline of Freshwater Ecosystems** by Janet N. Abramovitz

_____127. **Eco-Justice: Linking Human Rights and the Environment** by Aaron Sachs

_____126. **Partnership for the Planet: An Environmental Agenda for the United Nations** by Hilary F. French

_____125. **The Hour of Departure: Forces That Create Refugees and Migrants** by Hal Kane

_____124. **A Building Revolution: How Ecology and Health Concerns Are Transforming Construction** by David Malin Roodman and Nicholas Lenssen

_____123. **High Priorities: Conserving Mountain Ecosystems and Cultures** by Derek Denniston

_____122. **Budgeting for Disarmament: The Costs of War and Peace** by Michael Renner

_____121. **The Next Efficiency Revolution: Creating a Sustainable Materials Economy** by John E. Young and Aaron Sachs

_____120. **Net Loss: Fish, Jobs, and the Marine Environment** by Peter Weber

_____119. **Powering the Future: Blueprint for a Sustainable Electricity Industry** by Christopher Flavin and Nicholas Lenssen

_____118. **Back on Track: The Global Rail Revival** by Marcia D. Lowe

_____117. **Saving the Forests: What Will It Take?** by Alan Thein Durning

_____116. **Abandoned Seas: Reversing the Decline of the Oceans** by Peter Weber

_____**Total copies (transfer number to order form on next page)**

PUBLICATION ORDER FORM

NOTE: Many Worldwatch publications can be downloaded as PDF files from our website at **www.worldwatch.org**. Orders for printed publications can also be placed on the web.

_____ _State of the World:_ **$13.95**
The annual book used by journalists, activists, scholars, and policymakers worldwide to get a clear picture of the environmental problems we face.

_____ **State of the World Library: $30.00 (international subscribers $45)**
Receive _State of the World_ and all five Worldwatch Papers as they are released during the calendar year.

_____ _Vital Signs:_ **$13.00**
The book of trends that are shaping our future in easy-to-read graph and table format, with a brief commentary on each trend.

_____ **WORLD WATCH magazine subscription: $20.00 (international airmail $35.00)**
Stay abreast of global environmental trends and issues with our award-winning, eminently readable bimonthly magazine.

_____ **Worldwatch Database Disk Subscription: $89.00**
Contains global agricultural, energy, economic, environmental, social, and military indicators from all current Worldwatch publications. Includes a mid-year update, and _Vital Signs_ and _State of the World_ as they are published. Disk contains Microsoft Excel spreadsheets 5.0/95 (*.xls) for Windows.
Check one: _____ **PC** _____ **Macintosh**

_____ **Worldwatch Papers—See list on previous page**
Single copy: $5.00
2–5: $4.00 ea. • 6–20: $3.00 ea. • 21 or more: $2.00 ea.

$4.00* Shipping and Handling _($8.00 outside North America)_
*minimum charge for S&H; call (800) 555-2028 for bulk order S&H_

_____ **TOTAL** (U.S. dollars only)

Make check payable to: Worldwatch Institute, 1776 Massachusetts Ave., NW, Washington, DC 20036-1904 USA

Enclosed is my check or purchase order for U.S. $_____

☐ AMEX ☐ VISA ☐ MasterCard _____
Card Number   Expiration Date

signature

name   **daytime phone #**

address

city   **state**   **zip/country**
phone: (800) 555-2028   fax: (202) 296-7365   e-mail: wwpub@worldwatch.org
website: www.worldwatch.org

Wish to make a tax-deductible contribution? Contact Worldwatch to find out how your donation can help advance our work.